No-Secrets Leadership

James Jeray

authorHOUSE®

AuthorHouse™
1663 Liberty Drive
Bloomington, IN 47403
www.authorhouse.com
Phone: 1-800-839-8640

© 2011 James Jeray. All rights reserved.

No part of this book may be reproduced, stored in a retrieval system, or transmitted by any means without the written permission of the author.

Published by AuthorHouse 12/14/2011

ISBN: 978-1-4685-0593-1 (sc)
ISBN: 978-1-4685-0592-4 (e)

Library of Congress Control Number: 2011961438

Any people depicted in stock imagery provided by Thinkstock are models, and such images are being used for illustrative purposes only. Certain stock imagery © Thinkstock.

This book is printed on acid-free paper.

Because of the dynamic nature of the Internet, any web addresses or links contained in this book may have changed since publication and may no longer be valid. The views expressed in this work are solely those of the author and do not necessarily reflect the views of the publisher, and the publisher hereby disclaims any responsibility for them.

Table of Contents

An Institution In Need Of Change 1
No Magic Answers 9
Leadership as Service. 15
Communication 25
Motivation 35
Providing Feedback 47
Change Management 57
Trust and Risk 65
By the Numbers 73
Putting It All Together 83
About The Author 91
References 93

An Institution In Need Of Change

Why is there Dilbert? Or more to the point, why has Dilbert become so popular? How can a cartoon about bad morale and bad treatment at work by bad bosses develop such a widespread following? Take a walk through most offices and you'll see copies of the strip pinned or taped to the walls and Dilbert calendars on the desks.

A large part of the reason for its popularity is that, as outrageous as some of the situations are, they can hit very close to the truth. For a long time Dilbert's creator Scott Adams has been receiving suggestions by e-mail from people who experience examples of "laughable" leadership in their jobs everyday. With little exaggeration or embellishment on real life in the office, Dilbert has become an outrageously successful industry with comic strips, books, calendars, coffee cups, action figures and posters. It also has become a shorthand expression for poor management – "I work in a Dilbert company."

The humor (or sarcasm) of these comics is aimed directly at management. As a manager myself, I can see the humor, because I too have a boss. But I am torn between appreciating the strip as I laugh along and wondering why it has to be that way. I certainly have tried very hard over the years not to become the pointy-haired boss.

But the popularity of Dilbert, followed up with the popularity of the television series, "The Office," is only one indication that the problem of poor management is widespread. Each week in the business sections of newspapers people write letters to advice columnists asking how to deal with bad bosses or how to correct a situation of poor treatment. Typical headlines read: "Tyrant Boss calls for a little Diplomacy" or "Advice on Handling an Idiot Boss" where the columnist states his belief that about one half of us work for people he classifies as idiots. Other articles discussing how to deal with a bad boss use words like power freak, dictator, and even psychotic to describe the inhabitants of the corner office.

Would such books and columns exist if positive role models for management were plentiful or if letter writers felt that they had an opportunity for a fair hearing by bringing up these problems in the workplace? The opposite seems to be true. People are treated badly or neglected at work. Many develop the attitude of putting in their time and saving their energy for after-work activities. Finding someone who actually respects the boss for the job he or she is doing has become more and more rare.

Though this may be true at the front line levels, don't the better leaders, the ones we can respect, rise to the top? Unfortunately the national business news highlights almost weekly extreme cases where the company leadership is so focused on their own perks and job security that laws are broken and charges filed, while employees are left without jobs and retirement funds. Many of these top echelon leaders are so self-absorbed that they have little time or energy left to be good bosses. Ben Stein writing for Yahoo! Business calls this situation a national disgrace.

What effect does this have on employee satisfaction and productivity? In 2004, a Monster.com survey reported a level of 86% dissatisfaction with the current job, but this is a job-search website so it may be skewed toward people already looking for a change. Another survey by a more disinterested source in 2005 reported job satisfaction below 50%, down from 59% ten years earlier. Another source reports overall satisfaction at 50%, down from 79% in 1985. A 2009 Conference Board survey reported 45% satisfaction, while in 2010 Manpower reported 84% of employees planned to look for a new position within the next year, up from 60% in the prior year. More recent surveys confirm that the situation is bad and getting worse. In addition, reliable surveys and studies consistently show that the number one factor driving job satisfaction is the boss or immediate supervisor (over 40%), followed by the workload (around 25%) and then compensation (less than 20%). Negative boss behavior is also cited as the number one reason for a company or department to seek union representation. All this information taken together paints a dim picture of leadership in business and reinforces the need for change.

I have seen managers in their fifties scared to give their bosses bad news, that is, to tell them the truth. They emerge from meetings complaining of having been beaten up or humiliated. Some companies apparently believe that above average pay and benefits justify this treatment. It's as if they are bribing people to stay in this negative atmosphere and put up with the abuse. When you see union workers on picket lines, negotiations may be around better pay and benefits, but you can often see deep in their eyes the feelings of revenge for years of poor personal treatment.

So what can we do about it? Attempts to develop better leaders have inspired a myriad of quick fixes, academic articles, management workshops, and books and tapes on leadership, management, and all their aspects and subcategories. Where are the results? Despite a constant flow of books, articles, research and seminars giving leaders the "secrets" to success, America is creating more Dilbert companies.

Calling people "associates" instead of employees at some companies is supposed to send a message of mutual trust and respect. But later when those same employees are routinely treated poorly or hear themselves referred to in financial reviews as headcount, it serves to reinforce the difference between words and actions, giving them even more reasons to distrust management. It takes more than changing vocabulary to change the habits and the climate. No wonder a recent survey revealed that more than half of today's workers think their company spins the truth to make the leadership look better, and nearly 1 in 5 workers believes their employer is routinely not truthful.

For upwards of 30 years, consultants, academics and former CEOs have been publishing ideas about trait theory, behavior theory, contingency theory with combinations and hybrids of each. They have offered dynamic collaboration, the paradigm effect and Theory Z. They have addressed in detail leadership, motivation, change management, and a host of computer assisted integration programs to help everyone work better together. Yet there has been no significant change in complaints about negative boss behavior, unfairness, favoritism, dishonesty, and idiocy. In fact, all indications are that it's getting worse.

During the 1990s, the leadership of Jack Welch, CEO of General Electric, was held up as a model. A summary of his philosophy included that he required each of his divisions to be number one or number two in their respective industries or else he sold them off. In a similar vein, they would periodically review personnel and replace the bottom ten percent by performance. This approach is more in line with cleaning out the office refrigerator than with running a company and being a great leader. We should not judge leaders by their ability to inspect and discard. We should judge them by their willingness to own and their ability to fix problems. Jack Welch was held up as a model because he was successful in making short-term profits in very good economic conditions, but was the company better off after he left? Lately business writers are beginning to look at his legacy more critically. If leadership were as easy as jettisoning the deadweight, there would be no more need for leadership books.

The only real answer is to ignore all of the proposed secrets and get back to the basics. It is a disgrace that recent generations have had to tolerate this kind of treatment at work. The next generation should not! I have spent over 40 years leading people in groups of two or three to over 150 – not General Motors by any means, but I was always in a position to stay close to my employees and my customers, able to see firsthand what is going on. Feedback from both has been consistently positive. Along the way I have had time to experiment and learn from two different sources. I have learned what works from the theorists who have done good research, and I have learned what does not work from the jerks I have had to work for and my observations of many others. Bad examples and bad role models are easy to find. A negative experience or bad example can often be turned into a positive learning experience.

Most people want to be liked and respected. Most leaders would care if they knew that the majority of the workforce was talking negatively about them behind their backs, thinking that they are incompetent or worse. Of course it's nice to be liked and respected, but that isn't enough to justify a new approach. Justification comes from the fact that there is a cost to doing it wrong. Studies have shown that leadership problems lead to reduced performance and increased turnover. If you are not a good manager your best people are the first to leave, because they are the ones who have the easiest time finding another job. Others may not quit, but will lose enthusiasm, applying only the effort it takes to meet minimum acceptable standards. They will spend the day thinking about things other than doing the job right and satisfying the customer, things like plans for the evening or looking forward to the weekends. Multiply these effects by all of the poorly run companies in the US and it causes a considerable drain on the economy as a whole. Poor managers at all levels undermine the ability of corporations to be competitive and provide jobs. Effects on the stock market, the loss of jobs to overseas options and the trade deficit are among the results. Taken as a whole over the entire economy, it causes major problems.

The real answers can be found in those fundamentals, things like basic motivation theory or appropriate use of management sciences, that are violated daily in companies big and small. Most of the managers running these companies or the departments within them have received some instruction in the basics. MBA courses require an understanding of these and other subjects on the theoretical level, but somehow these lessons are forgotten or disregarded under the pressure of everyday business. When people are hired as managers or promoted they may assume that they are already fully qualified in terms of their leadership knowledge and abilities. They believe they already have all the answers and the promotion is a long overdue recognition of their superiority. These new managers function by making things up as they go along, trying to adlib their way through each new situation, or by observing available role models, picking up both the positive and negative behaviors and assumptions. These people will keep Dilbert and its imitators popular for decades to come. (Pointy-haired bosses breed more pointy-haired bosses.)

Sometimes it's the people with the technical skills who get promoted. The best salesman becomes the sales manager or the best programmer becomes the project leader. But relationships change when someone is promoted from within the ranks. It is different and awkward dealing with those who were once your peers. Sometimes it's the people with the charm who get promoted. They are good looking or smooth and have a certain political skill that gets them liked and noticed by the decision makers. But this charm is not going to be very useful in dealing with their new subordinates if they don't know what they are doing. Some get by for a while, even getting the next promotion by treating their bosses well and coming off like a dictator to the rest.

Many people want to climb the corporate ladder and are willing to make the personal sacrifices it takes to get to or near the top. Of these people no one wants to be regarded as a bad boss. But there are so many out there that Dilbert is everywhere in the workplace. What goes wrong? Do they just get so caught up in the action that they forget the fundamentals? The only way to become a good leader is to minimize the distractions of the latest fads and secrets and get back to the basics, and in that way to become the opposite of what is satirized in the comics, on television and in the movies; and the opposite of what you see all too often on the job. The real secret to leadership is that there is no secret.

This book is intended for those who are serious about developing their skills and making good decisions as leaders and managers and are looking for guidance on how to more quickly develop into a first class business leader. This book is targeted at those people who read the news or look up the ranks within their own company and see so many negative examples of leadership and don't want to become one, who have the right values but too few examples of how the tools of leadership should be used to support those values. There are a whole lot of bad bosses out there. What do you need to do to not join their ranks? Why would anyone who has ever worked for a bad boss want to become one?

What follows is a brief, but systematic review of the basics, the daily work of leadership, presented in a fresh and accessible way. It's not that hard when it's understood and kept in perspective. The chapters are arranged so that each builds on information presented earlier. Some of the areas to be addressed include:

- There are no magic answers; the magic is in the basics not in the silver bullet from the latest management book. It's human nature for people to search for the easy answers. Despite the periodic release of the next magic tool or technique, those easy answers don't really exist.

- Since the leaders do not do the work directly, their role in the organization can be puzzling. What value-added services do the leaders provide, and how does that inform their behavior?

- Results come when people clearly understand business needs and respond appropriately. Leaders must skillfully communicate objectives, listen, and motivate.

- Leaders need to check progress and make in-course corrections. Their people must be properly recognized for doing well and also given feedback both when they err and when they succeed.

- Change is constant and the employees are the ones who will implement the changes. Leaders must be adept at managing the message and the technical side of change.

- Since leaders can't do it all themselves, yet remain responsible, a clear understanding of the art of delegation is required. The ability to delegate requires trust and the willingness to take risks.

- Hand in hand with delegation goes measurement of results. Measurement requires the proper use of analytics, management by the numbers.

- Finally it's time to put it all together, using the individual techniques as pieces of an overall system or philosophy to guide managerial behavior.

I do not intend to enter into the debate about the distinction between managers and leaders. I leave that to others who see value in it. In fact I sometimes use the terms interchangeably. At the most basic level leadership or management should be viewed simply as the process of getting the job done by influencing others. The number one responsibility of leadership in business is to get everyone to really care about the customer and the quality of the product or service you deliver, whether it be to a consumer, another company, another department within the company or the next person in the process. Then leaders help identify and resolve problems with the current operation, learning from workers, customers, and other leaders, while looking out for the strategic and environmental challenges ahead and planning to overcome them. It's not just giving orders or selling a vision. Real leaders, great managers, help people grow. They leave a company or organization in better condition than they found it.

Many workers are raised in households where the message is passed on that the boss, the manager, the leader, the company are considered natural enemies. This is probably typified by, but not restricted to, a union shop mentality. The supervisor or manager often represents all of the negatives of the company: the bureaucracy, the oppression (through rules and policies), and the built-in power imbalance. This adds one more dimension to the difficulty of the relationship. New supervisors or managers may have good intentions, but with no role models and very little training or practice for the position and responsibilities, it can be an uphill battle. The company can make them a supervisor or manager, or even a vice president, by title but it can't make them a competent leader or manager. Over the long run it takes no more time and energy to be a great boss than it does to be a bad one. It takes time and practice, but there are no secrets or easy answers. That approach has been tried – without success.

No Magic Answers

A major problem with management in the US is that, as a reflection of the rest of society, there is a general reluctance to get back to the basics. Instead managers tend to seek some magic answer. "If only we knew the secret, we would be successful without putting in a lot of effort." There seem to be as many books about business quick-fix solutions as there are diet books. Not surprising - both involve the same dynamics, a straightforward solution which takes patience and discipline to execute. The real secret to losing weight is to eat less and exercise more; the real secret to leadership is practicing the basics of business management. Both are easy to understand, but hard to do.

Even though avoiding the basics yields little lasting improvement, the sentiment remains that there must be an easier way to get results. Executives and consultants talk of quantum leaps and step-level changes and look for techniques or programs to provide the needed boost to their company or department. This seems to be an attempt to get the work out without having to put the work in. Cynics within the companies quickly recognize these efforts as another case of "the flavor of the month" and haul out the appropriate Dilbert cartoon to post. In reality, truly successful companies, like Toyota, routinely make small rather than large system-design changes. They recognize the value of reducing the number of steps a worker has to take to perform a particular task. They learn from making small, incremental improvements.

This quick fix approach is often derived from the work of competent and sincere scholars or consultants who have their conclusions over-simplified. In other cases, authors realize that most executives don't have the patience for a long implementation. If business leaders are looking for the magic pill or silver bullet for their careers or organization, new or repackaged techniques are sure to sell if they are marketed well.

The problem is often not in the program, but in the implementation. Most consultants, academics and theorists who develop these models and write the books truly believe in the effectiveness of their product and have research to back it up. Although there are a few who might advertise it as a magic answer, in fact most warn that it's not a quick fix, and that their program requires dedication and patience. Still, with that latent enthusiasm for the next big thing, it is not unusual for another program to become a fad, as CEOs make headlines by announcing to the press that the company is adopting this particular "new initiative." What may be a basically good program like Six Sigma becomes for some companies more about marketing than about results. Most companies have come to recognize that a single technological solution alone will not improve a process and that a single program will not improve the company, but it doesn't seem to keep them from being lured in by the latest fad. Failures come from the belief that little efforts will yield big results.

As I look back over a 40-year career in business, I remember many such programs. Most should sound familiar to anyone who has worked for a large company or read professional journals during that timeframe. Some have become passé while others are still going strong. Each can boast of examples of companies that have had great successes with the program, but many other companies have failed or given up often after a great waste of time and money. (The dieting parallel keeps recurring.)

Some well known examples are: MBO (Management by Objectives), Deming Quality, TQM (Total Quality Management), Process Re-engineering, ISO 9000, Theory of Constraints (TOC), Lean Operations, Process Re-engineering, Six Sigma, and the Balanced Scorecard.

Others programs that have been promoted and have achieved a certain level of widespread recognition include Activity Based Costing or Activity Based Management, Economic Value Added, supply chain optimization and a host of specialized software applications. Among the latter are ERP (Enterprise Resource Planning) - (preceded by MRP and MRPII), APS (Advanced Planning and Scheduling), RFID (Radio Frequency Identification systems) that are replacing optically read bar codes, WMS (Warehouse Management System), TMS (Transportation Management System), CRM (Customer Relationship Management), the 8D Problem Solving System, AIDC (Automatic identification and data collection), and data mining. It's an alphabet soup of hope for struggling firms.

The list goes on and on. There are books and conferences, seminars and software, consulting practices and college courses built around many of these depending on the depth of the theory and the momentum of the movement behind it.

Most of these "solutions" are not bad. Many are well thought out and well researched. Good research goes on all the time on motivation, strategic planning, sales, change management, and how to improve organizations. As a result, the understanding of the practice of management and the information available in textbooks are superior today to that of the 1960s. The only way to stay current is to look for the important articles and not be distracted by the fads. The worst effect of the "latest new thing" approach is that it keeps the real work from getting done. It becomes a distraction and further problems arise from the overblown expectations that people place on them.

In my experience, what they have in common is that in one way or another they draw on the basics. In fact, recent studies have shown that most of them share a consistent emphasis on customer, vision, process, teamwork, quality and continuous improvement.

Clearly, success from any of these programs is not quick and easy. For them to be effective it takes a thorough understanding of the program and a commitment to it.

It is critical that companies choose the right one or two. Some can be used together successfully, like Six Sigma and Lean Manufacturing. If a company makes the choice based on good research and a good understanding of their own problems, they are off to a solid start. If instead they pick one based on a magazine article that highlights its success by another company or based on an announcement by their main competitor, it could be a mistake.

So, if we define the first requirement as getting back to the basics, the second is commitment. Most of these initiatives are complex and demanding. Commitment must come from top management. Otherwise the words and actions (especially recognition systems) don't agree and any initial momentum evaporates. They must be committed to the entire program for the long term.

Some companies fail because they don't commit to the entire program. Instead of seeing the program as an integrated whole, they "cherry-pick" the parts that are most appealing. In Deming Quality, for example, they want to produce fewer defective products instead of inspecting out the defects at the end of the line, but they don't want to recognize that the ability of the line worker to affect quality is limited by the systems that are set up by management. Despite warnings that they are ineffective, they resort to slogans and exhortations urging the workers, constrained by these limitations, to work smarter. None of these techniques work unless the company is willing to make the system, process, and culture changes necessary to support them. I was once invited to tour a production plant that built a sub-component for the company's main product. From the beginning of the tour, my group was told how quality and waste reductions were engineered into the process. On the next to last stop of the tour we were shown the hospital, the place where units that failed the final inspection were reworked. It was quite crowded. The last stop was a dock filled with finish product waiting to be shipped because the main plant was already backlogged and was not accepting additional deliveries until they caught up. It was clear to the tour group that quality was not engineered into the process and that this plant, which was part of the total business, was working in isolation.

In addition to accepting the program as a whole, the second part is commitment to stick with it for the long term. A friend works at a company where the managers were given three different books over an 18-month period and successively told that each was the new management philosophy the company was adopting. Managers read the books and attended meetings about how the techniques or beliefs would be applied. A short time later they went through the same exercise with the next book. The reception for these new break-through theories cooled as managers became more cynical and top management's credibility eroded.

Not all magic bullets are high tech. As opposed to many of those products listed above, others fall more into the category of soft side, behavioral science techniques. The list includes such things as team building exercises, leadership training, and inspirational activities, developing a mission statement or becoming a learning organization.

"Let's take the whole department on an adventure course," the manager decides. So everyone is off to the woods to climb log ladders and swing from trees. They spend the day together cheering each other on and brainstorming how to solve obstacle course problems. They may do trust-building exercises where they take turns falling backward to be caught by the awaiting team. No one is dropped and everyone seems invigorated. In another case the company may hire a motivational speaker to address the leaders or even the entire company at an off-site meeting, sales conference or annual meeting. The speaker is animated on stage, tells some great stories, perhaps leads the audience in the company cheer and instructs them to go out next year and do even better. (In the 1980s executives paid to attend seminars where they were encouraged to squawk like chickens to increase their productivity.) These are just a few examples of fads that sweep through the business world from time to time, not to mention the meetings and training sessions that arise from the latest book that the CEO may be reading on improving morale, lowering turnover, increasing the energy of the workforce, addressing people's weaknesses, playing to their strengths, or energizing everyone to have more fun at work.

These types of activities usually experience problems with relevance and half-life. Such activities and initiatives are rarely subject to the same cost justification standards as other organizational spending. Unlike most other expenses, they are not challenged to determine if the payback exceeds the cost. How are people's behaviors going to change, and how does that behavior change translate into profits? Will the experience result in more satisfied and productive people and a better-run organization? Are the investment of money in fees and travel and the loss of the participants' time justified? When you solve non-business problems away from the office, how does it relate to solving business problems in the office? Is it really going to fix problems we have and raise performance? Only the best managers spend time thinking about these questions.

Half-life refers to the tendency for the impact of the experience to decay over time. The trick used by the purveyors of these methods is to survey people immediately after the class or exercise, asking, "How beneficial do you think it was? Were you very satisfied? Do you think you will do a better job when you get back to work?" In the exhilaration of the moment, people generally answer these questions very positively. Later they return to reality and the mundane issues of the workplace. How would they answer the same questions a week later or a month later? Were the enthusiasm and commitment and change of attitude engrained or does it quickly fade? Most studies show that the positive changes if any have a dramatic rate of loss. If people are sent individually, they return to their job energized but find everyone around them the same as before. They may try to share their enthusiasm and newly found insights, but everyone is busy and the new disciple is met with a certain level of indifference. "That's all fine, but we have work to do." It's not fair to expect a newly trained person to convert the rest, so they are left to maintain personal changes on their own for as long as they can. They may be reborn, so to speak, but this is not common. If the group goes together, the result may be longer lasting, because they can remind and reinforce each other about shared experiences and learning, but unless there has been a complete change in the process and recognition systems to support this intervention, the day-to-day tasks creep in and slowly push out the benefits.

The answer for these is similar to technological "solutions" in that they must be determined to be a part of the solution, not the whole answer. They must also be valid, in that they deliver what they promise. Then they must be implemented with care and commitment.

I hesitated to start this book with the negative message that all of these available solutions may be of little value, but wanted to give a dose of reality – there are no easy answers. Let's not approach management like many people approach a diet, knowing that the answer is in the hard work of eating less and exercising more, but then trying out every easier way that seems to come along in the form of miracle diets, pills, surgery or patches. The answer to losing weight is basic, but sticking to it everyday is difficult. You must execute the plan and not be tempted by the quick-fix books and products. You can buy the exercise equipment to assist with the plan, but if it's not combined with better eating habits or if it soon lies dormant in the basement, it's a waste of money. Likewise the practice of leadership requires sticking to the basics and if someone comes along with something that seems to work better, first make him prove it, and second adopt it to solve the problem it was intended to solve and not as a panacea.

Finally, there is one other vital ingredient to successfully implement any of these initiatives – leadership. They are not a substitute for the hard work required to manage a department or a company. First, distinguish between the pure management fad and good, solid research. Most in the first category are easily unmasked as repackaging of a few of the basics with lots of hype to try to sell it as a brand new concept. Others put a new twist on a combination of old ideas. Understand the choices enough to separate the substantial from the superficial. Then choose the right one; make sure it is proven and fits the problem; and be prepared to commit. Anytime you see the word "secrets," be skeptical. Don't be looking there for a remedy to the problems created by poor leadership. Close inspection usually reveals that the introduction of these tools and techniques has no causal relationship with improved business performance. There are no magic answers to competent leadership.

Leadership as Service

Every MBA and undergraduate business major learns about Douglas McGregor in an organizational behavior or basic management class. In a famous book written more than 50 years ago McGregor suggested that managers generally may be classified as either "Theory X" or "Theory Y" according to how they view the work relationship and the attitude and abilities of employees.[1] Theory X managers operate under the assumption that workers are basically lazy and incompetent. They need to be watched and prodded at all times to ensure the work is getting done properly (or at all). This assumption results in a strictly adversarial relationship – the boss tells you what to do and you do it – or else! It arises in part from an erroneous belief on the part of the leader that he is smarter, more talented, more experienced and more important than those he leads.

Theory Y managers view workers as able and willing to do the job and treat them accordingly. The underlying assumption is that each person plays a role on the team. The leader acts as a coach providing direction and training, but the game is won or lost based on the performance of the entire team. The leader guides and facilitates while others do the work. Rather than using the Theory X and Theory Y terminology, I prefer the terms Parental Leadership vs. Partnership Leadership. A parental leader uses the power of position, the manipulation of reward and punishment and sometimes threats or coercion to meet his objectives. Partner leaders believe the organizational objectives are shared by everyone and use the perspective of the position and experience to guide their teams to a successful result. Partner leaders are stewards of the resources entrusted to them by the owners.

---

1   That book was The Human Side of Enterprise and has been widely cited and criticized since.

The concept of service, or stewardship, is really the essence of the argument in favor of managing in one way and not another. Given that getting back to the basics is key to good leadership, the first of the basics is that leaders are servants of the organization. Philosophers have argued for centuries that the definition of the Good Life is one spent in service of others. Founders of religions offer the same advice. How does this apply to the areas of business and leadership? Developing a personal philosophy of service to others is explicitly opposite to the kinds of managerial behavior that make a company a "Dilbert company."

The reason companies develop bad environments is not that the leaders are stupid. Rather they have a few bad assumptions: that they got their job because they are smarter or cleverer than others or that, because they are the boss, they are more important than everyone else. Some even act as if they are the customer – expecting service from those who work for them. Their employees start doing things in certain ways because "it makes the boss more comfortable," or "the boss wants to see it this way." These are bad reasons to do anything in business. Customers do not benefit from the boss being comfortable, and customers are the people who keep you in business! Customer service, not boss service, must be kept at the forefront if any enterprise is to succeed.

Often these managers get carried away with the belief in their own importance. They begin to believe they have the right to spend shareholders' money on personal conveniences or that backdated stock options are an acceptable practice, because they deserve it. In the end, this thinking leads to jail time for some, but many, many others get away with it on a smaller scale and end up wondering why personnel turnover is high, why shareholders complain and why customers feel cheated.

About 25 years ago a book was published advocating turning the organization chart, upside down. The traditional view of an organization is one of a pyramid having a broad base representing the many line workers and narrowing toward the top where the president or CEO sits. To know who your boss is, just look up the pyramid. It's a standard chain of command based on models from the military or the Catholic Church, one person at the top with layers below to follow orders. Instead this new model advocated viewing the same pyramid on it's point with each individual layer looking up to see what they need to do to support the ones above (with the customers at the top).

A similar way to look at the organization using the partner leadership perspective is to ask what the jobs of each group are. Salespeople talk to and persuade customers; line workers produce the product or deliver the service; logistics specialists make sure those products and services are delivered on time; etc. These are the workers. Without them there is nothing to sell and no one to sell it.

What does that leave for management to do? Peter Drucker once wrote: "Management is a response to the people who do the work." Management is expected to organize the work, set goals, try to look into the future to anticipate market shifts or demand for new products, review the overall performance of the company to ensure they are making a profit (that is, staying in business), recognize good performance, coach substandard performance, and make a host of other vital decisions. They are not, however, making or selling the product, which is the main purpose of the enterprise. They are looking at the past, present and future to ensure a smooth and profitable operation. In a sense, though, everything they do is somehow in support of the people on the front line who are delivering the product or service to the customer, getting new customers, billing the customers correctly, collecting payments and accurately keeping track of them. The workers who touch the customers or assemble products or write computer code are the ones the business really depends on. Usually these workers are so busy doing what they do that they cannot also ensure they have the resources, information or perspective necessary to get the best results. Management, in support of the workers, provides resources, structure, communications, and perspective.

Resources may take the form of equipment, raw materials, information, buildings, office equipment, parking lots or computers. Structure and communications break the organization up into smaller pieces that must be coordinated at some level to work together. Perspective is the understanding of how it all fits together so that everyone is pulling in the same direction, the right direction.

Bosses go wrong when they miss the point of serving those who are serving the customer. Business is not about making an executive's job easier. It's about making customers happy by giving them what they need at a fair price. It's always about serving the customer. Without customers there is no reason to exist.

How can the role of the leader be better understood? It can be summarized as:

- spanning the gaps and giving perspective;
- defining and facilitating the work, providing direction;
- performance appraisal, recognition and developmental feedback;
- representing the workers to the higher organization, acting as ambassador to make sure they get the appropriate recognition.

Operational people, those making the product or delivering the service directly to customers, are confined, more or less, to their areas of specialization. Managers have the advantage of a higher or broader viewpoint. They get to see more of the playing field, the big picture. When they share this added perspective with workers, it allows them to do a better job, focusing on and aligning with the long-term goals of the organization. Often various functions must work together to get the best result. Many companies, however, suffer from a "stove pipe" or "silo" mentality where artificial, psychological walls separate departments. When each area is inwardly focused, paying attention only to its own needs and budget objectives, opportunities are missed. Results are sub-optimized due to natural conflicts. Sales makes promises that manufacturing can't meet. Engineering designs products that are too expensive to make. The savings by using slower modes of transportation are more than offset by inventory carrying costs. Everyone is trying to meet his own budget without regard to the greater good. Managers are responsible to overcome this general lack of communications and to use their broader perspective to coordinate and resolve issues that arise due to distance, politics, or parochialism.

Back in the 1980s a common exercise was for companies to establish a vision and a mission statement. Originally the vision was a word-picture of the organization at some future state: to be the top in some field or to grow in a certain direction, or even to transform the organization into something new. The Mission was the statement of what business we are in so that we don't get distracted or get lured into a business where we have less expertise. In the age of huge conglomerates, trying to be all things to all customers was a common problem. It is management's duty to define, communicate, track and redefine as necessary. If people aren't told the mission or vision, they must make it up on their own. On a department level, providing this perspective can be a small part of a manager's job, but at the enterprise level, it's critical.

W. Edwards Deming argued that 80 to 90 percent of defects were not the fault of workers. They must be attributed to the operational process, which is totally under the control of management. Employees who are following the rules will not produce a better product just because you punish them for defects or try to motivate them with rewards or cheerleading. The problems are baked into the machines or the work rules or the process. Think of it in terms of driving a car. If the manager does not make sure the gas tank is full or uses the wrong map or misreads the directions, the employee will not arrive at the proper destination no matter how hard he tries to be a good driver.

"It's all management's fault." I used to hear this from a particularly smart-mouthed line worker when I was running a department of about 140 people. I would walk through the area and ask how things were going and be told that they were all screwed up and that it was all management's fault. Here is how I responded. First, I would agree. Yes, it was all management's fault. After all, the job I was being paid to do was to keep the department running smoothly while meeting the needs of the customer. If something was not working properly, it was my responsibility. So I would say, "Yes, you're right. Now tell me the problem and how you think it should be fixed." Of course this was not the expected answer and it was certainly not the answer that many managers would have given, but it was honest and it showed a genuine interest in getting things back on track.

As it turned out, usually there was not a major problem. The guy was just having a tough day and needed to gripe to someone and knew that he could blow off some steam by blaming something on me. My response calmed him down a little, cleared the air and maintained the open communications necessary to surface real issues as they occur. It also helped reinforce the service ethic. If I had said, "No, it's the workers' fault for being lazy or resistant to change," or even implied this by my attitude, it would have had the opposite effect. The fact is that he was right. When viewed at the most basic level, what ever goes wrong on the job is all management's fault. It's a lot of responsibility. As an example, the University of Michigan publishes airline passenger survey scores each year. In 2007 they dropped significantly showing the worst customer satisfaction since 2001. The professor who was asked to explain the results said that despite some factors beyond their control, fuel costs and congested airports, the bulk of the blame must rest on the airlines' management. That was exactly the right assessment.

Subordinate development is also the job of the manager. As your boss, your growth and satisfaction are part of my job. The more successful you are, the better it makes me look and the easier my job becomes – but it's not your job to make my job easier. At the end of the day, the people doing the work provide solutions for the customer and must own those solutions.

Managers are obliged to observe each worker and give him fair, objective feedback. This may consist of praise for a good job and developmental feedback in problem areas. Employees deserve proper training, a job that gives them a sense of contributing, and regular feedback to reinforce or improve their performance.

Sometimes managers have to defend their workers against abusive customers. The customer is not always right. When they harass or intimidate your employees, it's time to suggest that they take their business elsewhere. It may hurt in the short term, but it will pay off later. You can't support your employees on one hand but turn a blind eye while others treat them badly – even if they are customers.

Finally a manager represents his employees to the rest of the organization, getting them the recognition they deserve and adequate resources (supplies, tools, computers, etc.) to do the job.

Stewardship, then, is taking care of the resources entrusted to you. The most important of these resources is the people. Other resources are used up in delivery of the product, whereas people actually grow and improve. Companies will often talk about people being their most important asset, but it's rare to see them living out that philosophy on a daily basis.

A good friend and career army officer told me of an incident that happened when he was stationed in Korea. Most people don't realize that when the Korean Conflict came to an end there was a cease-fire, but no formal peace treaty. Everyone there, especially in units nearest the border, was expected to be vigilant and ready for action at any time. A sergeant from this friend's battalion was ordered to drive from one of the northern camps near the DMZ to 8th Army headquarters in Seoul to take care of some administrative business. It was the dead of winter, cold and windy, but there was a division directive that all jeeps must have canvass and windshields stowed at all times to be ready for combat. The sergeant arrived at headquarters where he was unlucky enough to be spotted and questioned by the 8th Army Commander. The General asked him why he had driven approximately 30 miles in such weather with the windshield folded down, no roof or doors, exposed to the elements. The sergeant explained the policy. Later The Division Commander, a 2-star general, received a call from his boss in Seoul questioning whether there should be an exception to the policy for a soldier driving on the streets and highways on a purely administrative task in those conditions. The Division commander could have understood the call as a recommendation to consider the health and welfare of his soldiers – in civilian terms, to take care of the workers entrusted to his leadership. Instead he issued a new policy: "No jeeps will be driven to Seoul."

An issue in the literature during the high tech boom of the 1990s was how to manage a millionaire (those people who had stock or options from the founding of a company and technically didn't need to work any more). Other magazine articles since then have approached the problem of high turnover by suggesting treating knowledge workers as volunteers. Partner leaders apply this not in those specialized cases alone, but to workers in general. To get it right, managers must never forget that the workers serve the customer and managers serve the workers. By keeping this in mind, not only are they doing their jobs well, but they are simultaneously serving as examples of good service – practicing what they preach. The best managers pay attention to, even anticipate, the business needs of their employees. The job includes communicating, motivating, and giving appropriate feedback. How to do these well is the subject of the chapters that follow.

****

This customer service approach applies to job applicants as well as employees for the following reasons.

There are people out there who need a job and the company has a position to fill. When we have something that others need, in the broadest sense, they are our customers. So why don't we treat job applicants like customers?

In business there are two kinds of customers, those who make a single purchase and those who will make multiple purchases over time. In the case of the repeat customers, you want to treat them well every time to develop brand loyalty. They will not be going to your competitors if you treat them well. In the case of the single-contact or infrequent customer, it is important to treat them properly to elicit good word-of-mouth advertising. Despite the fact that you may not see these customers ever again or at least not for many years, you want them to tell their friends that it's a great company to do business with.

Now read the last sentence and substitute "applicants" for "customers." Don't you want the same things from them? You want their friends to find out that even if they didn't get the job, it's the kind of organization that treats you with respect and appreciation. They may not have been a fit, but their friend might be the superstar you need to fill a key position. For the potentially successful applicants, don't you want to begin building loyalty to your organization from the beginning? The time to start building that loyalty is not on the first day of work or at the first formal expectations exchange but at the very first contact. Applicants are advised that they have only one chance to make a good first impression. The same is true of employers.

Treating an applicant like a customer does not just apply in tight labor markets. The best people can find jobs in both strong and weak economic times. In a good market they have choices. You decide to hire them and they decide whether to accept the job. In slow times they may not currently have choices and decide to take your job but to keep looking, figuring it's better than nothing. (How long would your business last if your customers considered your product "better than nothing" or a temporary solution?)

A second reason to treat applicants in this way is that a customer service attitude cannot be turned on and off at will. If your employees are in the habit of treating applicants well, the state of the economy becomes secondary. The process and level of care are consistent.

The final reason is that it's not that much harder or more expensive than what you are doing right now. I once had an applicant tell me on the drive back to the airport not to worry about whether I could match his current monetary offer. He really wanted to work in my department and would probably accept any reasonable offer. All we had done was pick him up at the motel, rather than having him take a cab to the office; spend a little extra time showing him around town, the place we would be asking him to move if he got the job; give him an agenda showing who he would meet with and their role in the department; make sure that interviewers were on time and if not, make sure he was not left alone to sit waiting and wondering what was next; and finally tell him that we would get back to him as soon as possible, appreciating that this was an important event in his life. By his response I assume that this treatment compared favorably to every other company he had applied to.

He was treated like a customer or guest. He later became an excellent, loyal employee. If I needed some extra work in the future I didn't have to ask twice. And his friends were calling, which reduced my future recruiting costs.

✳ ✳

Communication

The first requirement of leadership as a service is communication. Like it or not, leaders set the agenda. They control the communication, not just in terms of calling the meetings, but in terms of encouraging by their actions and reactions good, constructive exchanges. Communication skill is vital in business, just as it is in social situations and in all of life. Communication is the concept of getting a thought or idea from one person to another accurately and completely. The idea might be the details of an important project or simply where and when to meet for lunch. When communication fails, there may be arguments, misunderstandings, costly errors, confusion and a host of other problems. How many plays and movies over the centuries have been based on the comic or tragic results of a message not getting through or being misinterpreted? Communication failures have been the source of problems, frustrations and worse since the dawn of civilization.

I will break the topic into four areas: sending the message (speaking), receiving the message (listening), the choice of how to send the message (medium), and the importance of promoting open, honest communications. The first two are so interactive that it is difficult to separate them completely. Each medium has distinct strengths and weaknesses. Finally, developing the proper environment is critical to getting the information you need to make good decisions.

A common communications model is shown below. In each interaction there is a sender, a receiver, a message and a medium. It is important to the sender to get the message to the receiver. In business, the receiver must assume it is important to understand the contents of the message. Both are motivated to make the process work. The sender "encodes" the message, usually using words (and gestures and facial expressions). The receiver must then "decode" the message by understanding the words in the way the sender intended. Between the two is a lot of interference potentially blocking or distorting the message. When the message is received, the sender should seek feedback to check for accuracy.

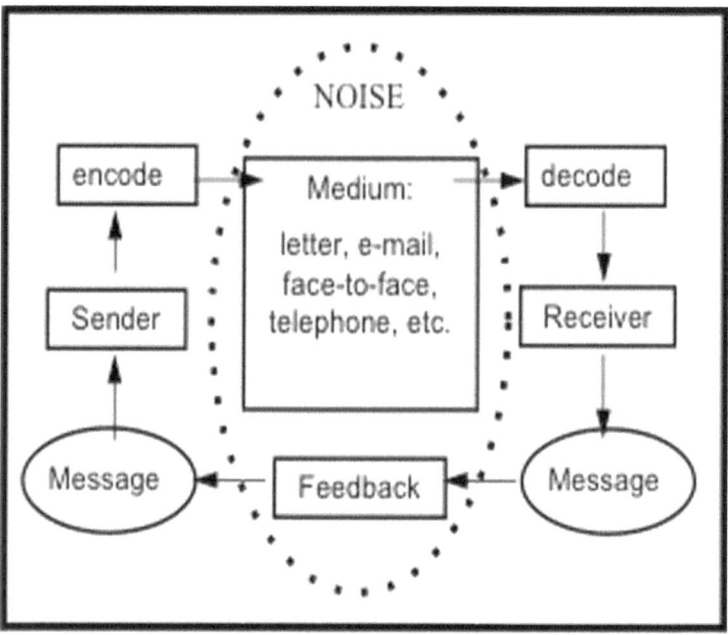

You have a picture or idea in mind that you want to convey to someone. In brief, you need to get information where it will be used. Often wrapped up with the information are your needs, expectations and feelings about the situation.

A skilled business communicator covers the following:

- subject - what is it about,
- scope - what's included and what's not,
- facts - what, where, when, who, and sometimes how,
- feelings - why is it important? What does it mean to me? What does it mean for you?
- desired outcome - what does it look like when it's accomplished?

A skilled business communicator does it in a way that is understandable:

- using common vocabulary,
- avoiding jargon or acronyms that may be unfamiliar,
- being organized and staying on the subject.

A skilled business communicator looks for understanding and agreement:

- asking for feedback,
- asking for agreement or commitment,
- scheduling follow-up discussions to review preliminary results.

Since the manager controls the agenda there are a few other things to consider in sending the message: consistency, overreaction, honesty, and choice of words.

Consistency of message is very important since your actions can quickly undo all your well-intentioned words. How does an organization react to cost cutting measures when they see the CEO flying everywhere in the corporate jet for "security reasons," the board or leadership team having special off-site meetings or golf outings? Even if the spending is not personal in nature, perceived inconsistencies can arise. Do department heads commission professional videos for a one-time showing at a large employee meeting? In many cases the message of this movie is a vague pep talk to work harder or smarter. These slogans and exhortations, as Deming called them, usually have no lasting effect, and many will see the underlying message, "they spend thousands on a video and at the same time expect me to watch every nickel and dime!" Actions speak louder than the words. What does the annual report look like? Is it a tasteful and modest presentation of company results, or is it a major production with glossy pages? I have seen a company spend money to use a copyrighted photograph (in lieu of free materials) on the company website while trying to get the employees to cut costs. I have seen the same company spend in excess of $50,000 to fly in a motivational speaker to address upper and middle management and then send the same managers back to their departments with instructions to keep the costs down. Don't think that the word of these costs doesn't get out. Usually the assistant, media liaison or marketing manager who is asked to make the final arrangements is so appalled at the inconsistencies that word is bound to leak. News of this apparent hypocrisy is far more easily spread than the message that the leaders intend.

Consistency over time is also important for credibility and acceptance. If the message has changed, explain the reason for the change (new legal situation, new competitive information, new business strategy, etc.). Don't just change the message.

"Leaders may forget the true impact of their words and actions, and they may assume that what they are hearing from followers is what needs to be heard."[2] Power of position causes some strange reactions (or overreactions). There is a joke about the CEO who asks for a cup of coffee and someone goes out and tries to buy Brazil. Sure this is an exaggeration, but it shows the natural tendency of everyone to try to please the boss, and it happens at all levels. Honest efforts to "exceed expectations" coupled with a poorly communicated message may result in a great deal of wasted time and resources.

As far as routine honesty is concerned, this hardly needs mention. Honesty is required to build the loyalty and confidence essential to any organization. Furthermore, full disclosure is preferred to under communicating. It is usually better to say too much than to say too little. Left to their own imaginations most people tend to come to the scariest conclusion, the worst-case scenario. For one thing, it's human nature and for another, it's always more exciting to spread a really exciting story about how we are all going to lose our jobs than the boring alternative that may be closer to the truth. If you as a leader do something and the reason is not clear, people are left to speculate about your motives. You walk through the shop and ask how a certain machine is working and you may be accused of considering changing the machine or a procedure. I once ran an operation with overlapping shifts. On my birthday I decide to bring in cookies as a treat for the whole department. As a gesture of recognition and appreciation to the people who started at 4:00 a.m., I arrived at 4:00 so that they would get the freshest cookies instead of the leftovers as so often happened. Instead of returning home, I went to my office to begin my regular workday a few hours early. To me it was fairly innocent, but to them it was a very unusual situation. I heard later that one or two workers on the first shift were saying that I had come in early to spy on them. After I got over my disbelief, I met with all the people on the shift to clarify my

---

[2] Bennis, Warren G. The Seven Ages of the Leader. Harvard Business Review (January 2004) p. 51

motives (and to remind them that problems with performance were not handled through spying or anything like it).

Words are powerful. Consider the expression "union organizing drive." The implication is that the company was *disorganized* before the arrival of the union. Consider your words to ensure you are not misinterpreted. This reinforces the importance of the feedback loop.

Finally, much has been written about how to run successful meetings. The above hints on individual communication can provide a simple guideline. Start with an agenda defining the subject, scope and desired outcomes. Get participants to share facts and feelings, staying on the subject. Make sure everyone understands. Get feedback from everyone, even by drawing out responses from reluctant participants. Get agreement, make assignments and schedule a follow-up as necessary. Sometimes it's smart to get even more feedback after the meeting asking one or two of the participants how they thought it went and what they think will be accomplished.

Having made so much of the importance of feedback, the subject of listening naturally follows. "The problem of managers not hearing what staffers are saying – in spite of good intentions usually – is endemic to corporate life"[3] It is difficult to treat listening as a separate activity. In any conversation or meeting you act as both sender and receiver of information or feedback. But I would argue that listening skill is the most important. If you don't communicate clearly the first time but you listen to the feedback, you will detect any misunderstanding in time to back up and correct it.

Agreement and commitment referred to earlier is not "OK, boss." To that you respond "OK to what?" The response should be "OK, I'll do X by Y." If X and Y match the message, then you're confident. If there is a discrepancy, you still have time to fix it before anyone's time is wasted. In this way your listening reinforces your message.

But haven't we been listening all our lives? What's the big deal?

Listening is not the same as hearing. Remember, between the idea or picture in the sender's brain and the transfer of that exact idea to the receiver, there is a gulf of noise or interference and potential misunderstanding. There are distractions, physical noise or other activities that catch your attention (someone walking by, the TV, e-mails popping up), and psychological noise (your other thoughts, moods, feelings). "Not right now, I'm busy!" Your prejudices, background, experiences, culture

---

3   Stengel, James R., Dixon Andrea L. and Allen, Chris T. Listening Begins at Home. Harvard Business Review (November 2003) p. 106

may cause you to interpret ideas or words differently. Often people are caught daydreaming or composing their response or defense to what is being said without really listening. All these can block the message or lead to inaccurate, faulty understanding of the speaker's intent. The idea is lost or different, and problems arise. In some cases the misunderstanding can be relatively harmless and easily cleared up, in others it can lead to conflicts or costly errors.

To overcome these problems requires the understanding, practice and preparation involved in Active Listening, sometimes called Reflective Listening.

Using active listening, one tries to create an atmosphere where your counterpart is encouraged to express ideas, feelings, needs, or to propose a solution to a problem. It is listening while using neutral summarization, and frequent feedback. It is listening for the whole meaning, what is said and the feelings behind the literal message. Here are some guidelines.

1. Stop what you are doing and look at the person.

2. Pick up on the non-verbal or tone-of-voice clues, the feelings of confidence or insecurity, worry or annoyance. In some cases it might be more appropriate to address these issues first. Respond to a guarded statement with, "It sounds like you may be concerned about hurting my feelings [or upsetting me] but things can't be fixed unless we discuss them openly."

3. Feedback the feelings throughout the conversations: "It sounds like you're really frustrated by the [blank] policy [or process]".

4. Paraphrase and ask for clarification (perception check): "I think I hear you saying…" Then take it to the next level: "Does this mean that you think we should scrap the whole project [or other conclusion]?"

5. Keep it neutral to minimize defensiveness or conflict. Describe feelings by name or cite descriptions of behavior: specific and observable words or actions without attributing motivation. Use "I" statement when describing your reaction. Instead of "You're really making me mad" say "I'm feeling angry about some of the things you are saying." Instead of, "You aren't making any sense" say, "I'm having trouble figuring

out where you're going with this." Stay calm, managing your own reactions. If both are looking for a workable solution, this approach will work. If someone is trying to bait you into a fight, you'll drive him crazy.

6. Continue to probe. Try to paraphrase the assertions your conversation partner is making. "In other words, ..." or "Do you mean...?"

7. Stay focused. One technique is to parrot back the words the person is saying to you to show you are paying attention. To do so accurately, you must pay close attention. (Do this only in moderation.)

8. Reduce internal distractions. Studies show that a person can talk at about 100 to 170 words per minute. A person can accurately listen at a rate of more than 600 words per minute. That leaves a lot of room for distractions: thinking about what you want to say next, remembering an even better story than the one being told, reflecting on your feelings, letting your mind wander. All of these interfere with effective listening. If necessary jot a quick note to help you recall a relevant thought that occurs to you and then quickly refocus on the other person's points. Your turn to speak will come. The more intelligent a person is, the harder it may be for her to take the time to listen. Patience may be overcome by the desire to get to the answer more quickly. Input from others may be dismissed or undervalued especially when the manager is used to being right most of the time and has had good results by trusting her instincts and doing things her own way.

The choice of medium is not totally straightforward either. Should you have a face-to-face discussion, call on the phone, send an e-mail, or write a letter? Each has advantages and disadvantages.

A face-to-face conversation is more personal. It is preferred when conveying sensitive or personal information. You can get immediate feedback and be more confident that your message has been received. You have the benefit of observing body language and facial expressions. It's more spontaneous but usually less organized. (That's why it's important to bring notes to or even rehearse a very important meeting, such as disciplinary action or a job interview.) In a face-to-face conversation it is easier to stray from the subject. It is also subject to the moods and distractions of each participant at the time. Ideas may be omitted or not thought of until later.

Telephone, like face-to-face, is more spontaneous and personal. It has many of the same disadvantages plus the fact that non-verbal clues are lost. It is possible to be a little more organized though, referring to notes or the computer screen without seeming rude. For the same reasons it is easier to become distracted, not having to make eye contact.

A letter is more formal than e-mail, but both are similar in that the writer has a permanent record of what was said. This may be good or bad. Even erased e-mails or deleted files can be retrieved. Preparation and organization are enhanced. You have the ability to edit or choose the right words. These media are not immediate and can be read at a person's leisure (with fewer distractions), considered and reread to ensure understanding. The organization and many requirements of a complex project or request can be captured in one place for later reference. On the other hand, the opportunity to express one's self non-verbally, to show humor and other emotions, or to pick up on non-verbal clues from others is lost or greatly diminished. Feedback, commitment or agreement is delayed and must be handled in other ways. Finally, it is difficult to ensure someone has received and read your letter or e-mail.

Even with all of this in mind a good manager will not settle for less than open and honest, two-way communications. This does not happen automatically. In fact, it's the natural tendency of employees to keep a low profile, to be defensive, to be careful what they share. The balance of power is weighted against them.

It's too easy for the manager to create an atmosphere where communications range from guarded, to outright withheld, to bordering on dishonest. "I am constantly surprised at the frequency with which chief executives feel threatened by open challenges to their ideas, as though the source of their authority, rather than their specific ideas, was at issue."[4] People don't want to rock the boat. They are afraid to be the bearers of bad news when they see previous attempts to tell the truth met with a "shoot the messenger" reaction. I once heard a vice president while delivering a written report to his boss, a top-level manager, suggest that we just "slip it under his door and run." Another manager from a different company

---

4 Zaleanik, Abraham. Managers and Leaders: Are They Different? Harvard Business Review (January 2004) p. 81

commented, "If you could just show the CEO this daily report, he would understand, but no one wants him to know how much [time and money] we are spending on this activity." Ken Lay, chairman of Enron when it collapsed used as his defense that he didn't know what was going on in his company. If that was the truth, whose fault was it, if not his own? In contrast, I have had employees bring suggestions to me, criticize my decisions and even yell at me out of frustration. In the latter case, the employee came back later to apologize, but I thanked him for letting me know how he honestly felt. I don't think I would have gotten another piece of honest feedback, if I had ignored or punished these people. If people cannot or will not give the manager information he needs, how is he going to make good decisions or initiate necessary changes?

To be an effective leader, it is critical to be a good communicator. Based on the amount of guidance and number of tips available, it should be clear that this is not a simple task. For some people it comes more easily than for others, but it often takes years of practice to become really proficient. The combination of speaking, listening, choosing the appropriate medium, and putting it all together in a non-threatening way that encourages feedback or follow-up is a difficult task; but it's key to the rest of the skills in this book: motivation, constructive feedback, change management, trust building and accurate measurement of results.

The key then is to a) create an atmosphere, which encourages good, even confrontational communications, b) be a good communicator to pass along the information people need, and c) practice good listening skills to really understand the feedback and to know for sure that your message has been understood.

Motivation

The theory and practice of motivation seem simple, rewards for doing the right thing and punishment for doing the wrong thing. If it's so simple, why do so many corporate incentive plans malfunction, producing the wrong behavior or undermining cooperation?

My grandfather was a milkman many years ago working for what was at the time a large company. He had a horse and wagon and would deliver dairy products door to door, selling, collecting on bills, and picking up the empty bottles to be returned. It was good work and allowed him to support his family, and a couple of other families during the Great Depression when any job was hard to find. One day when he was driving near the border that separated his route from one of his fellow drivers, he noticed his colleague stopped at the side of the road so he took a slight detour to see if he needed help. When he got closer he noticed that other driver was not in trouble but had stopped next to a storm drain in the road and was pouring cottage cheese into the sewer. My grandfather was puzzled and asked the man why he was doing that. The man reminded him that there was a contest for the milkmen at their depot. Whoever sold the most cottage cheese would receive a cash prize. He explained that he was going to buy all of the cottage cheese himself, dump it down the sewer, and win the prize which would be enough to pay for his share of the cottage cheese with a little bit left over. In the process, he would earn a reputation with the boss for being a great salesman – a reputation he felt would pay off come bonus and promotion time. Is this the behavior the company sought when they set up the contest?

Almost everyone I know who has worked in business for any length of time has an equally outrageous story of an incentive plan gone bad. As hard as management tries to design a good program, if they are not extremely careful, someone will figure out how to play the system, often finding counterproductive ways to take advantage of loopholes. In other cases, the workers will easily see the flaws in the program and chalk it up as another stupid management attempt to manipulate the work force.

Here is a more recent example from a large trucking company. The long-haul drivers would leave home on Sunday to make the first delivery of the week on Monday morning. Usually they were on the road for most of the week and did not expect to see home again until Friday night or Saturday. Understandably it was difficult for them to leave and natural for them to procrastinate. Some would hang around longer than they should, resulting in the first delivery of the week being late. Customers were unhappy and productivity was adversely affected. Each group of 40 or so drivers had a supervisor and the company began tracking the instances of late Monday deliveries by each supervisor. One enterprising supervisor began coming to work on Sunday afternoon and calling each driver at home to see if he had left yet. If the driver was on the road, all was well, but if he was still at home the load would be late. In those cases, the supervisor would go into the company computer system and update the Monday delivery to a Tuesday delivery. Because the entry was done before Monday, it would not register as a late delivery, just a schedule change. If those drivers happened to make it Monday, it would show as an early delivery. If they delivered on Tuesday they would still be on time, at least according to the system doing the tracking. This supervisor made no attempt to contact the customer or counsel the drivers, so the dual problems of productivity and customer service were not addressed. The official reports, however, showed that his group of drivers had the fewest late deliveries on Mondays. His peers knew about this activity, but nothing was reported to upper management. Imagine the effect on morale among his fellow supervisors when this person who was cheating the system was singled out for a special award from the company president!

A final example comes from the world of sales. A man selling coffee to grocery stores had a quota to make and was having trouble making sales. His pay was contingent on his making that quota. The quarter was coming to an end and the company would be required to report earnings.[5] Knowing that he was running out of time, this salesman submitted orders in the names of some of his larger customers for the additional cases that

---

5   One well-documented shortcoming of the US economic system is the disproportionate weight given to quarterly results. Companies fail to make appropriate long-term decisions because of this constant pressure on the short term. Companies emphasize quarterly performance and end every quarter with a last-minute scramble for sales.

he was expected to sell. He ordered them to be shipped by railroad, the slowest form of transportation available to him. By the time the orders arrived, he was betting based on years of experience that these customers would be just about ready to reorder. He would then surprise them with an unusually prompt fulfillment. If not, he had to cancel orders that had already been shipped, but still got credit for the quarter in which the orders were originally entered.

These are examples of motivation gone wrong - well intentioned, but poorly designed systems yield poor results. Such situations are more common than expected. The lesson to be learned is that company-level motivation systems often fail, first because if there is a loophole, somebody is going to find it; and second, because many don't follow the basic theory of motivation which applies to both groups and individuals. To get the desired results you must be very careful when designing reward systems. The challenge then, is to set up a system that is not easily cheated or manipulated. Problems occur when the rewards become the prime focus for the workers (or even for executives), more so than doing the job right. Problems occur when you disregard the basics.

Many people have studied the principles of motivation over the past 60 years and their findings can be boiled down to some common sense guidelines that apply on both the group and individual level.

The first principle of motivation is that people are motivated internally. You can't motivate others; they motivate themselves. The best you can do is to create conditions where they are more inclined to be motivated, but ultimately it comes down to an individual choice. Attempts to push too hard or force people to behave in certain ways are seen as manipulative; and manipulation doesn't strengthen relationships, it tears them down.

Different theories of motivation tend to agree on a few key points.

- The reward must be valued by the individual and seen as proportionate to the behavior (or effort) required.
- The reward must be credible and the intention to deliver it believable.
- The desired behavior must be clearly understood.
- The person must believe he has the ability to do what is required.
- There should be a close temporal link between the behavior and the reward.

If these conditions are met, chances are good that the system will meet its objectives. If they are not, it will probably fail.

First, the reward, what is offered as an incentive, must be valued enough by the person that he is willing to adjust his behavior. People are complex and have different internal drives, so communications, especially listening, is key. Errors occur when the system designers expect everyone else to be like them, to have the same tastes, the same emotional requirements, the same expectations and the same values. An executive might appreciate tickets to the opera whereas a line worker might much prefer tickets to an outdoor or hunting show. Furthermore, there are some people who would be equally happy (or unhappy) with either. I read an article about a discount store that gave clerks an employee discount on everything except food and clothing. Their clerks came from some very poor neighborhoods and saw little benefit to the discount since what they needed most was food and clothing. The discount was not a motivator and not effective in minimizing turnover. Group rewards must usually be broad enough to appeal to most individuals within the large group. To get around this some companies offer cafeteria rewards where people earn points and use them to shop from a catalog.

Money would seem to be the easy answer. Everyone values money. Unfortunately that's not always the case. The extra cash may not justify the amount of extra effort required. It is not uncommon for hourly workers to turn down voluntary overtime (at 1.5 times their pay level) to spend more time with family or to attend a special function. Many people have taken a job for less pay because they were willing to trade the additional dollars for a better lifestyle. Think of those long haul truck drivers mentioned earlier, or of new consultants who spend weeks at a time at a client location living out of a hotel room. Despite the good pay that goes with some of those jobs, people leave in large numbers to satisfy other personal needs. Money is not always the easy answer, because its value may vary under different circumstances.

On the other hand managers make a mistake by undervaluing certain rewards. I'm sure you have read of instances where workers were angrily protesting because the company eliminated a small but highly anticipated reward, like a Christmas turkey. Workers felt the company was being cheap and arbitrary and was not respecting their wishes. The managers seem surprised at the reaction. To them the Christmas turkey was something minor, not worth the trouble.

The biggest mistake managers make is to assume everyone else has the same tastes, needs and motivations as themselves. They are led astray by two seemingly sensible pieces of wisdom. The first is the golden rule: do unto others as you would have them do unto you. The second is the idea that not treating everyone equally is to show favoritism and is not acceptable. In fact especially concerning informal recognition, that which is not set and administered by the organization, the best practice is to treat others as they, not you, would like to be treated. Understand that each person is unique and important. Preferences vary from person to person. It's necessary to know your people well enough to determine individual preferences. After all, to go to the trouble of recognizing good work and not having it appreciated is wasted time at best and possibly even counterproductive. You offer a worker something she doesn't value and her justified conclusion is that you don't know her very well or don't care. As a result, you don't enhance motivation, and you may very well build resentment.

As mentioned earlier, money is not always the answer to motivational issues, and surveys have shown that many other forms of recognition are appreciated and can act as effective motivators. Books have been written with ideas of how to reward people without breaking the budget by using informal, non-monetary recognition. Employee surveys show time and again that sincere personal recognition from a manager or leader can go a long way toward keeping people motivated, happy and performing well.

In a well-known case from the 1920s, the Hawthorne Experiments, researchers wanted to test how increasing or decreasing illumination levels on the shop floor would affect worker productivity. They expected to see productivity increase with more light. In fact it increased when they improved the lighting and also increased when they decreased the lighting, until it became extreme. They concluded that workers were reacting more to the extra attention from the researchers than to the lighting changes. This shows the power of informal recognition. Attention from an authority, especially a direct supervisor, can carry more weight than many other factors in the workplace.

Informal recognition can also be personalized to a great extent. For non-monetary recognition some experts divide people into five general categories according to how they prefer to be appreciated. These categories are verbal, quality time, gifts, favors, and contact. The categories describe the approaches different individuals respond to and usually correspond to the methods they themselves use when showing appreciation to others. Much can be learned about people's preferences by observing them. Verbal people like to be praised in writing or in person. Quality time people feel appreciated when a boss or respected co-worker spends time paying attention to or interacting with them. Some people like to buy and receive cards or small gifts: a book, a pen, or a keepsake. Others would rather have someone do them a favor; recognize them by following up promptly on an issue or by offering to help reduce their workload. Finally, some people are more physical than others. A handshake or (literal) pat on the back means a lot to them.

Whether the recognition is public, at a meeting for example, or in private is also an important consideration. You don't want to "reward" a somewhat shy person by possibly embarrassing him with an announcement in front of a large group about a personal accomplishment, whereas others may feel that nonpublic, private recognition is not worth as much. Remember, everyone does not think the same way as his leader or manager.

Any reward must also be believable. If someone promises you something in return for a special effort, you must be confident that he has the ability and the intention to deliver on that promise. As a leader you must, in turn, have the ability to deliver on your promise if you are to be taken seriously. Usually individual managers do not have the authority to override corporate policies, for example granting an extra week of vacation or giving a pay increase at a greater than normal frequency. Permission from the human resources or benefits department or some other higher authority is required. A promise that in the eyes of the worker cannot be delivered on will not be effective. Likewise if a company sets up a program, but has built in a number of hurdles or technicalities, it will fail to motivate. This is especially true if some employees feel they have been cheated out of a reward based on past technicalities. I once worked with a person who left the company bragging that his new employer had offered a sign-on bonus that would "put all of my kids through college." It was contingent on him working there for a year, but his employment was terminated after 10 months. His friends later guessed that the company wanted him not for his skills, but just long enough to "pick his brain" for industry knowledge. How often can a company get away with pulling tricks like that before it affects their overall credibility? Those who see this sort of thing happening may fall back on the old adage: if it sounds too good to be true, it probably is. An unrealistic reward, even one valued by the individual, will fail to motivate.

Intention also plays a role. If the leader has developed a reputation for not keeping promises or for saying one thing and doing another, a promised reward will not act as a motivator.

Certainly if a manager is going to reward someone for performing in a certain way, that person must clearly understand what is expected. Don't leave it up to people to guess what you want them to do. Clearly state the behavior, results and conditions necessary for the reward to take place. Do you want people to show up everyday for work on time? Is a certain level of output from a machine the desired goal? Do you want a certain level of customer satisfaction? How will these things be measured? Do the measurements really reflect the desired outcomes or can the measurements be manipulated – as was the case with the supervisor of late-delivering truck drivers?

The employees must also believe they have the ability to do what is required, that they have enough control or skill to accomplish what is being asked. Some companies pay annual bonuses based entirely on the performance of the company as a whole. They reason that if everyone works hard, the company will do well and everyone gets rewarded. Especially in a large company though, an employee will quite logically conclude that a small error by the CEO or a slip and fall by someone else in the parking lot will affect his bonus in the downward direction far more than his daily efforts can influence it positively. Such a bonus becomes a reward for being employed on the day the bonus is paid and nothing more. It has minimal motivational value, except possibly for the top executives (who think everyone thinks the same way they do).

Companies or individual managers may set unreasonably high goals. Rather than looking for improvement in customer service surveys, anything less than a perfect score results in a call from headquarters. Serving the customer takes on the additional facet of subtly coaching the customer on how the survey is viewed: that totally satisfied means satisfied and an answer of only satisfied is interpreted as dissatisfied. The survey loses most of its meaning and usefulness.

Sometimes people feel like they just can't do it. Once the person understands what is required, he must believe that he is capable of doing it. If the goal is set at 500 per day and the best anyone has ever done is 300 per day, there will be no motivation no matter how tempting the prize or how much faith the worker has that it will be delivered. There is no sense in even trying for the impossible level of 500. The offer is more likely to discourage the worker convincing him that the manager doesn't understand the work well enough to set realistic goals.

Finally, timing is very important. If a dog owner comes home from work at 5:30 and finds that his dog has made a mess (probably several hours earlier), he may smack the dog. The dog is confused and will not associate the punishment with its earlier behavior, but will associate the smack with its owner coming home. The result is a dog that still makes messes, but fears the arrival of its owner. People are not dogs, but the principle is the same. If they can't make a clear, logical connection between their good performance and the recognition that follows, they will not feel motivated to repeat it. The time lag plays an important role in making this psychological link. If they think they are doing a good job, but have to wait and wait to hear anything about it, they may lose heart and stop trying so hard. Even if recognition eventually comes, it will be harder to link the reward with the previous behavior and the motivational value is greatly diminished. Some experts go so far as to recommend recognizing people for a job well done at least once a week – even if it's for something relatively minor. Still, this recognition must be sincere and tied to a specific action or result. Praise without real progress will have little effect, while ignoring real progress easily leads to low morale and even cynicism.

These are the basics of motivation and can be applied to most situations of both formal and informal recognition programs. Rewards must be sincere, timely, valued, believable, and linked in some obvious way to a realistic desired behavior or result. If these conditions hold, people will work to achieve the reward or positive feedback. If even one is missing, the individual recognition or company-wide program will be less effective.

Before closing on this subject let me cover some of the trickier areas related to motivation. These include promotions, the reward/punishment relationship, and the issue of re-engineering.

Promotions are a special kind of reward. It not only increases a person's prestige, title and privileges, but it often moves her into a higher pay range. A promotion, however, is a double-edged sword. It gives the worker an opportunity to contribute more to the enterprise, but also to do more damage due to the well-known "Peter Principle": where people are promoted for doing a good job until they reach the level where they no longer can do a good job and are then left in that job. They advance to one step above their highest level of competency. So promotions as a reward need to be balanced with the concept of promotions as an attempt to put the right person in the right job. The best salesman is often not the best sales manager, the best engineer is often not the best engineering manager, and likewise for other specialties.

Another caveat about promotions applies to managing younger workers. A person first arrives at work directly from school where he has been "promoted" every year since he was 5 years old. Unconscious expectations may be in place that if I don't get a promotion every year I have failed to deliver. Since companies don't have 35 or 40 levels and titles to fill a career with annual promotion, it is an unrealistic expectation that may need to be dealt with up front. Otherwise this expectation left unmet can lead to dissatisfaction and reduced motivation.

Related to the timing aspect of recognition is the fact that promotion systems often give credit for getting things started, but move managers out of the position of responsibility before any results from the change appear. So when the great new programs take off with a bang, the managers who initiated them are recognized with promotions. Later when they crash, the next managers are the ones who have to live with the headaches and sometimes the bad reputation of being the leader during the period of (pre-ordained) failure. Do you recognize people for starting a program, or for starting programs that are valuable and successful long term?

The flip side of reward is punishment. The same principles apply: timely, seen as negative (as opposed to valued), credible, and linked to some identifiable undesired behavior or result that was within the person's control or ability to prevent. Idle threats are as ineffective as unbelievable promises, but punishment in general has less motivational value than rewards and recognition. Whenever possible find something good to focus on.

Motivation should not be used as a substitute for process change. In the example above of the worker being asked to deliver 500 units per day when the going rate is more like 300, management is looking for a step-level change in performance. Unless the workers are participating in some kind of intentional work slowdown or other passive-aggressive practice, the improvement is very likely impossible under the current design. Such changes call for redesign or re-engineering of the process, which is management's responsibility to lead. Sometimes large improvements can be achieved if these are properly designed and implemented. The implementation, however, requires knowledge of change management, the subject of Chapter 7.

How wrong can things go when the systems are not set up and monitored correctly? In the army, transfer and accountability of property is a big deal. Each soldier has personal items to sign for such as a sleeping bag, backpack and a long list of other equipment for deployment to the field. Officers must also sign for all common equipment assigned to their unit including each bed, radio, desk, truck, generator – anything that can be moved that is not expendable. At the end of a tour of duty, it is all turned in or counted and signed for by the relieving officer. What is missing must be found, explained or paid for. There was the case of the army lieutenant who found himself short a certain $2000 radio relay unit in his inventory. His platoon had one on-hand but was expected to have two. His options were to do a lot of paperwork and explaining or come up with another radio. One day he secretly took an ax and chopped the good one he had in half. He instructed the sergeant to fill out the standard paperwork turning in the two halves as the remains of two separate units "damaged during a training exercise." At the end of his tour of duty he received top marks on his evaluation report from his commander, a man who obviously knew little about his values and methods, who inadvertently reinforced this negative (and criminal) behavior, and worst of all, sent the message to the lieutenant's contemporaries that similar behavior would be rewarded.

Motivation may not be as easy as it first appears. The truth is that it's not that difficult either. We reward what we value and people do what they are rewarded for. By carefully following the principles and anticipating problems, you can make motivation work for you and your company. Think about examples from your own work experiences or that of your family and friends. When individual motivation efforts or company recognition programs are less effective than they should be, the failure can usually be traced to one or more of these principles.

Don't misinterpret, though. It's not a game to be won or lost. A well thought out and well administered system of rewards and recognition makes the company stronger because the workers want to contribute. It builds a bridge between good results and good things happening to the worker, even if it's only a sincere and well-appreciated pat on the back.

This chapter is really about recognition and reinforcement. Motivation is the traditional term used to describe the formal and informal systems. The purpose of these systems should not be to inspire good performance or right behavior. Remember, a basic assumption must be that people have pride in their work and want to do a good job. Motivation comes from within. What do you get when you "speak softly and carry a big stick" or use some other heavy-handed motivational technique? At best you get compliance, people doing what you want them to do only when you are standing over them. That doesn't work over the long term. When they do that good job or get that positive result, it is part of the boss's job to notice it and acknowledge it – to keep them inspired, lest they choose instead to come to work and go through the motions, but get their inspiration from and apply their energy to outside activities, like sports or hobbies. How many children misbehave or act-out, because that's their way to get attention? How many spouses resent being taken for granted? Employees are human with the same needs and feelings.

When I started in my first job after leaving the army, I arrived on December 17. On Christmas Eve, only a week later, the president of the company walked through the office handing out envelopes to each person. It was the Christmas bonus. To my surprise, I got one too. As I said I had just arrived and was still in the orientation and training stages, as informal as it was. I received an envelope containing $25 in cash along with a handshake from the president. It wasn't a lot, but back then gasoline was still under a dollar a gallon. I was very impressed. I hadn't really done anything but be there, but I felt a much stronger sense of belonging. I'm sure the president and others were unaware of the full impact. I had only been there a week and in many ways still felt like a stranger. This simple gesture made me feel like part of the team. I remember that feeling to this day, and that early, positive experience lasted for many years. Later, when the company asked for a little extra time or effort, I gave it willingly, not grudgingly.

Providing Feedback

A good leader gives feedback to employees to improve performance or maintain good performance. Like incentives, rewards and punishments, feedback can be positive or negative. In either case following certain guidelines can increase the probability of having a productive discussion. In this chapter we consider how to give effective feedback, including how to structure the conversation, maintain a positive tone, and follow-up. This approach can be generalized to apply to many types of problems or to reinforce desired results.

Is it job-related? A wise human resources executive once told me that one of the first considerations when making personnel decisions should always be whether it is job-related. The primary reason for conducting a feedback or counseling session is to effect behavior. In fact one definition of leadership is the ability to influence people to act in a desired manner. For legal reasons as well as effective time management, however, the leader must distinguish between job-related behavior and personal preference. Many examples are found in the area of work habits, such as appearance or punctuality. Asking if it is job-related can help the manager avoid spending time on extraneous issues instead of those that affect the work being done.

An administrative assistant once confided in me that she was being counseled (scolded) for not coming to work at 8:00 AM. Instead she would arrive at 8:15, usually due to problems at home getting her family organized and out the door. I asked what work was not being done or what customers were being inconvenienced by this delay. There were none to her knowledge. Was she not working her full workday? No, she would stay an extra 15 minutes, or more if necessary, at the end of the day to make sure the work was completed. It was not clear to me what the business need was for her to be at work at exactly 8:00 AM, and why there was such a fuss being made about it.

In that example I only got one side of the story. Perhaps there were people in the department with critical work that had to be started in order to meet deadlines. Perhaps there were customers calling or being inconvenienced due to her arrival time. But the evidence I heard, and what I knew of the operation, indicated that the starting time was somewhat arbitrary and the energy being spent to fix "the problem" could have been more productively applied elsewhere. Not only that, but it was detrimentally effecting the communications and relationship between her and her manager. In addition, there is always the possibility of employees seeing it and taking sides. When it comes to blind enforcement of arbitrary policies, there are no winners.

This advice also applies to recruiting. Interview questions must be job-related to be legal. You can't ask someone whether they own a car, but you can ask if they have a reliable way to get to work. You can't judge a people on the basis of appearance, unless they are going to have face-to-face contact with customers, and even then it's a delicate area. Interview questions must focus on those skills, knowledge, and attributes required for the job and whether the applicant possesses them. Asking yourself the simple question of whether specific requirements are job-related saves time and possibly keeps you from being on shaky legal ground.

Once the performance or behavior has been identified and determined to be job-related, it is time to plan the intervention. It is important to confront performance that needs improving or behavior that is detrimental to the operation, but the word "confront" should not imply unnecessary forcefulness or lack of courtesy. The approach to be presented assumes that the employee wants to do a good job. Most people understand the level of their own performance and are unhappy about doing a bad job or slacking off. To them it's not about pleasing the boss or concern about getting in trouble; it's about personal pride. (This approach also works better than the alternatives with the few people who don't care about the job or refuse to give the needed effort.)

When corrective action is called for, there are three simple guidelines for developing the solution. First, maintain the person's self esteem. It's about the performance or the behavior, not about the person himself. You will be much more likely to get someone to try hard and to improve if that person leaves the conversation feeling worthwhile, capable and valued. A person who leaves the meeting feeling beat up or demeaned will be less cooperative and less inclined to make the changes necessary. You want the person to be energized toward better results. Second, it is important to really listen to the individual. By listening you will get clues about the receptivity of the employee as well as reasons for the problem and even possible solutions hidden in the responses. This is a prelude to the third prerequisite, which is to involve the person in finding a workable solution. Every story has two sides and every problem has multiple solutions. The right one may or may not be the obvious one. The best approach is to involve both parties. Full participation leads to better solutions and also increases the employee's feeling of commitment to the solution.

In summary, the guidelines are to maintain self-esteem, to listen to both the facts and the feelings, then to ask for suggestions and work cooperatively to solve the problem. It is then possible to develop a plan consistent with those guidelines to address and correct a multitude of problems. The conversation can be broken into five steps.

1. Explain the behavior or the performance in a non-threatening way.

2. Get agreement on the importance of the problem. Emphasize the business impact. Answer the question "How is it job-related?" to clarify the issue of why the change is important.

3. Ask for input in solving the problem, improving the situation, or maintaining the high level of performance.

4. Discuss various alternatives and agree on a course of action. Make sure to get closure: you will do this; I will do that, by when.

5. Set a follow-up meeting to review progress.

It's all about fixing the problem. You have certainly heard in the context of parenting, "Punish the behavior, not the child." The thought process is the same. Step one is not to accuse or badger. It is to state in a friendly, problem-solving way what is going on and to begin a constructive conversation to fix it. The point in Chapter 1 that many employees see the manager as the enemy can make this particularly difficult. The second step is crucial. Unless the employee agrees that the problem is important, he will not be inclined to make the effort necessary to correct it. Describe the importance in terms of how it affects the customers, business, his coworkers or his own ability to do his job rather than to say, "It's important because you'll be fired if it doesn't change." Listening to the other side of the story, to the words and the feelings, helps keep the conversation on a constructive path and also helps determine if he has agreed that it is an important issue. If agreement about the existence of a problem cannot be reached, there is little to be gained by continuing the conversation. Your employee will not be committed to changing something he continues to believe is not a problem. This will become clearer in the examples that follow. Steps 3 and 4 are the collaborative parts of the discussion, which ensure both ownership and a good, workable solution. Step 5 sets a date for the next meeting, which can follow very much the same format.

Here are a few abbreviated examples showing conversations between the manager (M) and the employee (E):

> M: Glad we could get together. There is something I want to talk to you about. I've noticed that you've been arriving at work five or ten minutes late for the past week or so and want to know if there is a problem. *This is not presented as an accusation, but just a matter of fact. The manager implies that she is there to help. (How directly the situation can be addressed may depend on the prior relationship between the two and the personalities involved. Each manager must know her people well enough to judge.)*

> E: I was late today, but here on time yesterday! What's the big deal! *By listening the manager hears the defensiveness. This should not be surprising.*

> M: OK, settle down. I didn't call you in to scold you. Yes, you were here on time yesterday, but today is not the first day you were late. I am beginning to notice a pattern and I thought there might be a problem that I could help you with. *Calm the discussion down, but stay on topic.*

> E: OK, so I have been late a couple of other times, but I still don't think it's a big deal. *See how the manager will not be able to get anywhere until the seriousness of the situation and the job-relatedness are agreed to.*

> M: Well, I'll tell you why I think it's a problem. There are customers at the counter when we open and the phone begins to ring. If we

can't take care of them efficiently, they will take their business to our competitors. You know that the two others can't do the work all by themselves. Even with all three of you here the opening surge of customers keeps things pretty hectic for the first half hour or so. *If the groundwork has been laid for this kind of business understanding in previous meetings and communications, this may be enough of an explanation. It also depends on the maturity of the employee, but this important hurdle must be cleared in order to move forward. Assuming sufficient discussion has taken place...*

E: Yeah, I see what you mean, but I just can't help being late sometimes. *At this point the manager hears that there is some underlying problem. The choice is to solve it collaboratively or take a threatening stance leaving the employee to solve the problem "or else!"*

M: Tell me what keeps you from getting here on time on those days. *She asks for participation and shows a willingness to listen.*

E: Well... *The employee goes on to explain a problem with the car, difficulty with other car pool participants, trouble getting the children to day care, unreliable alarm clock, or one of a thousand other possible reasons. By now the employee understands that the underlying issue, whatever it may be, is causing a problem, agrees that it is important and becomes a willing participant in the solution.*

M: That sounds like a possible cause of the problem. What do you think we can do about it? *The first suggestion may not sound like a plausible cause. In that case it is the job of the manager to use probing questions to arrive at the more likely underlying cause. Once a possible cause has been identified, the manager encourages the employee to start problem solving in a "what can we do" rather than a "what are you going to do about it" way.*

At this point the employee may suggest a number of solutions or may be stumped for an answer. The manager can suggest a number of other solutions. Perhaps the manager has the flexibility to allow the employee to start half an hour later in a slightly different role, or have someone on a prior shift work a little longer so that the overlap covers the time delay. In these "work habits" situations, it is usually the employee who has to do most of the changing. In this example the job-related problem is that the customers are lined up and potentially being disappointed by the service. It is in the interests of both to come up with a satisfactory solution. Finally a solution is agreed to.

> M: OK, we have agreed that you will arrive on time to serve the customers by going out today after work and buying a new alarm clock without a snooze button that has a battery option in case the power goes out and set it to ring 10 minutes earlier. I think that will work. Let's get together in two weeks to see how it's working for you. *The step of getting closure is completed and a follow up meeting has been set.*

The above example and solution may seem trivial, but the process will work for most any problem. An employee is not meeting reasonable production goals. State in a direct, but friendly way the problem and why it is a problem. Express confidence in the employee that he can improve performance. Analyze, brainstorm and solve the issues together. Perhaps retraining is needed. Perhaps he never realized the importance of the goal – thought they were suggestions and not measured objectives. Perhaps he used to hit the goals but has been discouraged by not receiving recognition for other contributions. Perhaps he has been involved in another project and his goals were not appropriately adjusted to reflect the reduced time available to do his regular duties. Perhaps he is being distracted by personal problems and needs to take some time off or get outside help to resolve them. Many of these can't be solved, and will in fact be made worse, by increased pressure from the manager. Many are beyond the ability of even the most perceptive manager to detect. A collaborative process is needed to get to the root cause of the problem.

Two weeks have gone by and it is time for the follow up meeting. The tone of the meeting is dictated by the results achieved. In case number one the problem has been solved or is improving.

> M: Thanks for stopping by. I wanted to follow up on our last meeting. I noticed that you have been arriving on time. It appears that the problem is fixed. Thanks for working this out.

> E: Yes, the new alarm clock is working out well. I also [the employee mentions another idea] and that seems to help too. I did come in a little late on Tuesday, but that was because of [reason] and I don't think it will happen again.

M: Well, nine out of ten days is much better and the customers are being served better, so thanks again and keep it up. *Manager has shown appreciation for the improvement and has expressed confidence in continued success. The employee knows that the manager cares about customer service and will be back if any other problems occur.*

What about the situation where there has been no improvement? There are two possible problems: the agreed upon solution is not working or the employee did not really agree to the importance of the situation. Sometimes it's just a matter of finding a better solution, which can be done using a repeat of the above conversation with the learning of the last two weeks added. More difficult is where the employee went through the motions at the meeting, but was not committed to the behavior change.

M: Thanks for stopping by. I wanted to follow up on our last meeting. I noticed that you are still arriving to work late. Over the past two weeks you came in late a total of four times. This leaves the customers waiting and frustrated.

E (1): Yeah, but I improved to six times being here on time! Isn't that good enough. *This guy isn't getting it! He thinks it's about arbitrary rules and not about customer service, which is vital to the business. Back to square one for the manager.*

– or –

E (2): Yeah, I bought the alarm clock and set it 10 minutes early like we talked. Then I tried 15 minutes, but no matter what I do I still can't seem to get here on time.

M: Well, you know this is serious. Is there anything else you can think of to fix the problem? *Return to brainstorming for solutions. Why didn't it work? What else can we try? Then agree again and get closure and set another follow up meeting.*

At some point this process has to end. Either the employee is doing the right things and exhibiting acceptable performance, or he is not. Managers have other things to do and can't be spending endless time on these confrontations. Where poor performance continues and the follow up meetings have turned into frustrating reruns, the employee must begin to understand that working in the job requires acceptable results. Timing may vary depending on the severity of the situation and the progress shown, but eventually the manager will tell the employee something like, "We have been working on this issue for quite a while and, although we have made some progress, your performance is still not where it has to be. I can only give you one more chance to improve. If we get together for the follow up meeting next month and this problem has not been corrected, I'm afraid I will be asking you to leave the organization." This is a tough conversation, but it is much easier when the manager has identified the problem and gotten agreement that it is unacceptable and has shown her willingness to collaborate with the employee to come up with a mutually satisfactory solution. Most important, the manager has always focused on the problem, rather than blaming or demeaning the employee, and has expressed confidence that it can be fixed. If it comes down to firing, some people are just not the right fit for certain jobs. They don't have the talents, skills, or motivation to be successful. They are not bad people, just a bad match for the requirements. Usually by the final conversation the employee has figured this out, at least subconsciously. The groundwork has been laid and the departure, though not a happy event, may come as a relief to both parties.

Note that your organization likely has a set of termination procedures based on legal or contractual requirements. Some, for example, may require a formal written notice. To meet these requirements, document the conversation and agreements after each meeting. In any case it doesn't hurt to write up the results of a meeting and have the employee sign a copy. It both documents the conversation and reinforces the agreement. Check the organizational guidelines and adjust the process accordingly.

Although this may look like a "cookbook" procedure, it needn't be treated as a formula or applied in a mechanical way. It can be especially effective when each situation, employee and problem to be solved, is treated as a unique opportunity for individual growth and development. Although these conversations are not pleasant, a positive result can strengthen the relationship between the employee and the manager.

The process is flexible and can be expanded to include improving already acceptable performance – "You are doing this, but I think you are capable of producing at a higher level, or contributing across a broader front," etc. It can be modified, as will be shown in a later chapter, to address department- or company-wide changes. Finally the same process relates to training.

Training is like counseling in that there is a behavior which the person needs to exhibit to be more successful in his job, but the new behavior requires development of a new skill or an understanding that the person does not currently have. Mastery of the skill will result in the ability to perform better. First, there are training objectives – at the end of this session the student will be able to perform a task or explain a concept or apply a theory to everyday situations. (Having a specific and relatively immediate application is what distinguishes training from education.) Next, the trainee must accept that the new skill will be beneficial and see the importance of the training. In some cases the trainee will not be able to master the skill right away, even with practice it's not getting any better. The instructor or coach and trainee can then collaborate to determine what actions to take to overcome the problem. Finally, scheduling a follow-up review for the new skills, check for learning, can make training more effective.

This technique is all about improving work habits and performance, which lead to satisfied customers and better company results. It treats the employees professionally and encourages people to learn from their mistakes. Other approaches may tend to intimidate them into feeling they aren't allowed to make mistakes, which saps creativity and the willingness to take reasonable risks. If in the end, someone loses a job, it's not seen as an arbitrary judgment; it's about a problem that both parties understood and accepted and which, for some reason, could not be resolved.

Using this approach will produce one of two results: better sustained performance, or the departure/reassignment of an employee who was not surprised by the decision and who feels little or no animosity toward a manager who made a fair and reasonable effort to resolve the problem. This is the proper purpose of giving feedback.

Many managers find it difficult to give their employees direct feedback. Disciplining an employee is tough. Firing someone is painful. It's only natural to delay a potentially unpleasant conversation for as long as possible. When performance slips, they turn a blind eye hoping it will fix itself. Sometimes this happens, but more often it only gets worse. Ironically, the longer the situation persists, the more difficult the confrontation becomes. The better a manager understands, the more he practices, the better he masters these techniques, the easier it will become. This is one of the main responsibilities of a partner leader, to help employees become more productive (and more promotable). You owe it to your customers, your employees and your employer to get it right.

Change Management

The subject of change has been at the forefront of business news and management training for the past three decades. In the 80s it was the need for businesses, especially in manufacturing and electronics, to change to keep up with advances in quality and efficiency by their Japanese competitors. In the 90s it was the Internet revolution. If a company didn't have a web site, it was falling behind. The speed at which computing power was advancing served as a constant reminder of how quickly any company could become obsolete. Many of the enterprise planning and integration tools referred to in Chapter 2 were being developed. When the "dot.com bubble" burst, companies still did not get relief from the need to change. Out-sourcing at home and abroad led to increased competition and the need to keep costs low.

The struggle to survive continues. From the most sophisticated industries to traditional, old-line companies, there are new innovations daily that can give your company a competitive advantage or allow the competition to leave you in the dust. By now it's a fact of life that all companies must change and be ready to change again on short notice to remain competitive. Today the business world is dominated by speed, connected by instant communications and kept current by real time reporting.

The biggest change has been the speed of change. The fact that companies must change has always been true, but now there is a shorter grace period to decide how to go about it. How many hotels are worried about hiring elevator operators? Instead they are concerned about the operation of their customer relationship management system or their billing system, or about how well their forecasting and revenue management systems calculate the amount and timing of discounts in order to achieve the right balance in their occupancy rates to maximize profits. Even to grow is to change, and it's been a long time doctrine of business that a company is either growing or it's dying. There is no middle ground.

Change is necessary to keep a business healthy, but there must be some balance. One hundred percent constant change is chaos, but no change at all is stagnation. There is a need to mobilize energy around what must be changed while maintaining smooth operation of the rest. This balance is one that every manager must be aware of to ensure the long-term viability of the enterprise.

There are many theories of change management to help companies who struggle with implementation, but they usually boil down to the fact that the success of any new process is equally dependent upon the strength of its design and its acceptance by the people who must participate in its implementation. Resistance from the people involved can undermine the best ideas. Since people naturally resist change, gaining acceptance is crucial. If the change effort stalls due to resistance from the workers, there is the danger of assuming that the idea was faulty and abandoning an otherwise sound approach in pursuit of an alternative that may turn out to be a dead end.

When it comes down to it, it is the people who must make the change happen. Getting buy-off from each of those people is critical to the success of any change program. Again, the challenge faced by managers is that everyone is different, and different messages and approaches will appeal to different people. Everyone wants to know, "What's in it for me?" They must accept the need for change and clearly understand what will be required.

One well accepted theory of change sets four conditions for success:

1. The people who implement the change must be sufficiently dissatisfied with the status quo that they are willing to seek something better.

2. The expected outcome or vision of the future must be clear. After the change is accomplished, what are things going to look like? This is sometimes referred to as the model.

3. What is the plan to get from here to there – the path to follow from the current state to the model?

4. Is it worth the cost – both the personal cost and the

organizational cost? For both the participants and the organization there is risk.

Change happens only when there is sufficient discomfort, dissatisfaction with the status quo. If I'm happy with the way things are going, I have no incentive to change and I will resist change because it makes my life more difficult and brings me no tangible benefits. The attitude will be, "If it ain't broke, don't fix it!"

Partner leaders as change agents must first deal with this issue of discomfort. It's said that no one minds change, but everyone resents being forced to change. By nature people will resist. The new way is, at least at first, less comfortable and less convenient than what people have successfully done in the past. Their personal history of success can be a difficult obstacle to overcome. Why should someone take the risk of changing a proven pattern for an alternative with an unknown track record? So what is really meant by someone not minding change but not wanting to be changed is that they must understand that the environment has somehow changed, and that this change will cause the old ways to fail. Then they must move beyond understanding; they've got to believe it, to really feel it!

In addition to the comfort with the traditional way of doing things, there is a fear of incompetence, a fear of being unable to perform new tasks in a new way or the old tasks in a different way.[6] Fear of failure or embarrassment can be a powerful disincentive to learning a new skill or trying a different approach.

The challenge is to develop agreement among the employees that change is necessary. This need can be made apparent by citing external threats to the company – if we don't change, these bad things are likely to happen – and opportunities – if we do change, these benefits will accrue. It's called the "survive and thrive" argument. We need to change to survive because of certain threats, and if we change we will be better off. By showing how the competition is winning business away because they can lower their prices due to a more efficient operation describes a threat of loss of business and loss of jobs. Leaders present the fact that the company must become more efficient in response to this real external threat. For example, we must buy a computer system to help schedule production of various products instead of making the changeovers in the

---

6   This idea is taken from Edgar Schein's work on organizational culture and shows that the model holds for all changes from the simplest day-to-day adjustments to a comprehensive changing of deep cultural beliefs and practices.

old way – on a regular schedule or by the "gut feel" of the foreman or some other traditional method. In addition, if we get this new system it will allow people to develop new skills making them more valuable (possibly higher pay for higher skills) and make their jobs more interesting and more secure. These and any other opportunities can be cited. As discomfort with the status quo increases, there is better acceptance of the need to change. A clear vision of the future may not yet exist, but doing nothing becomes unacceptable. This is a conclusion that must be reached by each individual, in some instances by the union leadership, and especially by peer thought-leaders and first level supervisors.

The computer system example is only one case. Substitute any type of change and the challenge is the same. If the leaders requiring the change cannot come up with persuasive threats and/or opportunities, perhaps they need to rethink the reasons for their own proposal. The example chosen though also highlights the fact that systems and processes within companies are interrelated. One change implemented will likely ripple through the organization either as a part of the plan or as a reaction to discontinuities resulting from changes elsewhere. That new scheduling system in the manufacturing area may affect employees and managers who work in adjacent or related areas like inventory control, purchasing, sales, and logistics.

Another example can be taken from the contract negotiations between the UAW and the US car companies in the fall of 2007. News over the four years since the previous contract had been growing more and more negative. Financial results were negative and market share was slipping on a quarterly basis. Toyota moved from number three to number two to number one in sales, successively passing Ford and GM. No longer the Big Three, these companies were being referred to as the Detroit Three. A change was needed on many fronts, but much of the news focused on the area of labor costs. Both the union leadership, who did the negotiation, and the employees, who would be voting to accept or reject a final contract, had to be persuaded that major changes were needed for these businesses to remain viable. In the previous year there had been massive workforce reductions through early retirements and buyouts. The union even reopened the contract to give GM and Ford a break on health benefit costs. In the spring Daimler sold Chrysler to a private equity firm. The level of discomfort was already quite high. The union leaders seemed to understand that it was not a matter of whether to "give back" but how much. Near the end of the opening rounds when talks were getting bogged down and GM union employees were working "hour to hour," the union called a strike. It was the first national UAW strike against GM in 37 years and was intended to send the company a message, but it likely sent their members a message as well. Everyone was surprised and despite the fact that it only lasted a few days, employee discomfort increased substantially. The GM workers agreed to the contract on the first vote, followed, reluctantly, by Chrysler workers and finally, smoothly by Ford workers. They agreed to what some called a revolutionary contract because the majority of workers clearly understood the threats and the opportunities, which had been emphasized in news reports over the past several years, and which they accepted as real. (Four years later, after two of the companies were forced into bankruptcy and bailed out by the government, all three agreed on the first vote to a contract providing profit sharing in lieu of guaranteed pay increases. This series of huge changes over four years required a high level of acceptance of the reality of the economic threats on the part of the union members and their leadership.)

Note the direct parallel to the performance feedback process. To get employees to improve, they must first agree that a performance or behavioral problem exists. To get employees to accept a particular department-wide or company-wide change program, they must first agree that change is necessary. The format is very similar, except that it is normally done at a group level.

Another key concept referred to earlier is the natural tendency for managers to assume that everyone else is like themselves, with the same preferences, tastes, feelings, fears and motivations. A manager can't sell the line workers on the need for change with the same arguments that were used with financial executives. Tailor the message to the audience, but make sure in all cases that it is honest and above-board.

Assuming you can raise enough dissatisfaction with the current situation, you must be ready with a possible solution – "Here's where we are; here's where we need to be." Contrast the current state with a desired state. Show how the new model will deliver better results, overcome threats, and take advantage of opportunities. Everyone must understand this model. Sometimes the model may be a diagram or a new organization chart. It may simply be a description in words of a better process, method or state of the business. It may require a demonstration of software or a mock-up or simulation of the new information system. Keep it as simple as possible, but make sure it is thorough and clear. The purpose of the model is to let everyone involved form the same mental picture of what things will look like after the change has been accomplished.

The next step is to develop the plan. What are the milestones and timelines to reach the desired state? For small changes the plan may be obvious. For example, changing business hours to better serve customers may only require a new arrival time for some of the people who directly serve those customers. Larger scale changes may involve multiple project plans, cross-functional teams, or outside consultants, and may take months, or even years, to complete. Bringing on line a new computer system to replace an obsolete, legacy system that supports the entire company is a daunting task. A reorganization to decentralize a large, international firm would require a complex plan. These complex changes are not the kind to play by ear.

Especially when making complex changes, no matter how detailed and carefully planned they may be, some items are bound to be overlooked. That's when the universal understanding of the model comes into play. If everyone knows where the company is going, whoever notices the oversight or discrepancy can take immediate action to correct it and get things moving smoothly again in the right direction. Each participant knows the desired outcome and can realign even the most minor factor. Without this understanding, people are guessing, and either will not detect omissions, or will not know what to do to get things back on course.

Finally consider the cost. The model and plan to get there will add requirements to the budget. If the solution proposed is too expensive, a new one must be found. (Perhaps the employees, who understand and accept the need for change, will have some ideas.) In any case, it would be foolhardy to push the company to the brink of bankruptcy by implementing a plan that was developed to make it more competitive.

Using a simple analogy, change management is like planning a vacation:

1. (Discomfort/Acceptance) You don't want to spend your vacation sitting at home; it's not exciting enough or restful enough. You are on vacation and expect to have fun. The whole family agrees. (Otherwise this is the first problem to overcome.)

2. (Model) You pick a destination and timeframe that will satisfy the needs identified in step one: theme park, beach, cruise, spa, golf resort, etc.

3. (Plan) You plan your itinerary, pick dates, decide whether to drive or fly, make reservations, etc.

4. (Cost) You check the budget to make sure you can afford it. If not you need to modify the plan: choose another, more reasonable destination or reduce the length of the stay. If it's affordable, you finalize the plan.

It is important not to skip steps or get them out of order. A new model without a plan will appear confusing or intimidating to everyone. They will not understand how to get there or will think it can't be done. A plan without a clear vision or model will be puzzling causing people to wonder why are we doing this or where are we going? Without employee acceptance that change is needed and their commitment to that change, the leaders' efforts will be a waste of time.

Finally, in change management as in any other important area, the leadership must lead. They cannot sit back and give orders, expecting the rest of the organization to go through painful changes while they fall back into their routine patterns. This is Partner Leadership, not the parental model of "do as I say, not as I do." As was pointed out in the communications chapter, the actions of the leaders carry a message that supersedes all the meetings, posters, speeches and e-mails. Leadership in change requires painting a clear picture of the need, the solution, and the plan to get there. The picture can be clear, however, without all of the details filled in. Involve everyone to the extent possible in fleshing out the basic plan. This will raise commitment. Communicate: ask people to do something, ask for ideas along the way, and report on progress. Support the change effort with recognition for milestones met, goals achieved, and outstanding performance. Remember, real change only happens when there is a visible commitment from the top.

Trust and Risk

To become effective as a partner leader requires a great deal of trust and confidence – trust in people and a generally positive opinion of the nature of people, and confidence in your own judgment and abilities. Without these traits it is difficult to delegate responsibility or conduct a performance feedback session in a collaborative way. The potential results are worth the risk.

There is an expression, "Don't take it personally, it's just business," but a well run business is a personal experience for all involved. It is not some cold bureaucracy demanding compliance. It's people working through and with others. If you throw out some of the bureaucratic rules and policies, you aren't losing control; you are throwing out the coercion. Workers become volunteers. As such, they can choose to become personally committed to specific goals and will make extra efforts to achieve them. They stop watching the clock and begin to come up with ideas on the weekend or evenings to move the effort forward. The rewards are mutual. This sense of ownership leads to commitment, which leads to personal fulfillment, which leads to enjoyment. In the end, all parties win.

I was once in charge of a team of industrial engineers and logistics analysts. Knowing how highly technical people value continuing education and staying current in the field, I got permission to set up a training budget that differed from company policy. Instead of individuals having to justify each seminar they wanted to attend and having the request approved or not depending on short-term financial results, I assigned each member of the department a personal training budget. Each received the same budget averaging from two to three hundred dollars per month for the year. The amount was calculated and budgeted during the department's annual planning period, so it had to be approved only once. This amount was available for books, memberships, subscriptions, classes, or seminars (including the associated travel expenses). It was their personal training budget to spend as they wished. The only restriction was that they propose the use of the money during the annual review of their individual development plans. Not overly strict in its application, this program allowed them to choose a specific expenditure, e.g., joining a particular professional organization, or make a more general, plan such as learning more about finance and accounting by taking a night class or attending a seminar.

The system worked quite well producing a number of benefits. People gave more thought to their personal development. Managers did not have to spend time throughout the year managing each issue or approving each request. People were relatively frugal with the funds, treating them as their own. Individuals could get permission under special circumstances to go over budget, so it was perceived as fair and the money was not spent on trivial items. In addition, there was no "use it or lose it" attitude at the end of the year, because the people had faith that the program would be renewed. They understood that it was an exception to company policy, and did not want to appear to be taking advantage of the trust that was placed in them. At the end of every year the budget as a whole showed a favorable balance in this category, and everyone was satisfied with his or her training opportunities. The program was also presented as a benefit or additional selling point when recruiting new employees.

In one particular case, one of the people (with a PhD) was asked to speak at a conference in Spain. He recognized that he could accept and count the trip as a professional development experience covered by his training budget. The problem he came to me with was that the corporate travel group came up with an airfare costing $1500, but he found one for $600 on the Internet. He wanted permission to buy the cheaper ticket. This was a company expense but he was making the same decisions that he would have had it been his own money. He was given the responsibility for appropriate spending and went beyond what others might have to ensure the right decision was made.

This was not an isolated instance. In other cases people would survey their peers by e-mail to find others interested in the same seminar so that they could take advantage of group discounts. In many cases this was done without involvement of a manager (except possibly, as a member of the e-mail group).

The above is just one example of delegation with good results. Some would argue that such behavior might be expected from engineers with PhDs but the same does not apply to people who work on the line or behind a desk. I disagree. In some cases, the less authority a person expects, the more he seems to cherish what is given to him. I have seen people with desk jobs fight just as hard to clarify an error in a company phone bill as they would had it appeared on their home phone bill – as long as they know someone will back them up.

In many cases managers are so worried about their own careers or job security that they hesitate to trust anyone with any but the smallest decision. Their subordinates constantly complain of being micromanaged. This is the result of fear and ignorance and the outcomes are the opposite of those described above. The manager is afraid the workers will not take the responsibility seriously enough. He does not believe the employees are capable and is not willing to stake his reputation on their results; yet isn't that the definition of leadership?

Those who doubt the capabilities of their employees should pay attention to the conversations on Monday mornings about how people spent their weekends. They will soon gather a wealth of behavioral examples of what people are capable of doing. While away from work, they make decisions and plan where to go and what to do. In most cases they arrive at work telling what a good time they had, i.e., the success of these plans and decisions. Even if everything did not work out perfectly, they were usually able to make appropriate adjustments. They organize vacations or parties. Most pay bills on time and make reasonable financial decisions. They buy cars, keep them insured and rarely run out of gas. They raise children, plan meals, keep personal appointments, etc. These all seem like simple things, but each contains elements of those personal skills and characteristics necessary in business: planning, effective communications, organizing people and events, initiative, good judgment, and leadership.

Not only are they getting practice in these business skills on their own time, but they often will work harder on the weekends, on home improvement or playing sports, than they do on company time. Why? They have the responsibility to do it, and they try to do it right. They know the results will reflect on them. Most people take pride in their work when they own it. There are some exceptions, but I have found these to be few.

A number of years ago, I worked with a group that included some real outdoorsmen. The Monday conversations told about dragging ice-fishing shanties, which they had built themselves, onto the lake to spend the weekend fishing in the freezing cold. Another time they were deer hunting together. They must have gotten impatient because they devised a plan to line up and march through a swamp to flush the deer past their waiting buddies. (It didn't work.) When people like this act unresponsive at work, no one could call them lazy. There must be something about the set up – the system, the environment, or the management style – that causes them to react without enthusiasm, to go through the motions and not have their heart in their job.

In contrast, I heard of another situation from a line worker at a different company. He knew of certain workers who devised a contest to see who could get away with doing the least in a 40-hour period. The ultimate goal was to go for a full week doing nothing and not get caught. Rather than showing how you can't trust some people, this example only reinforces that if they are not involved, they may be motivated to find their own ways to get recognition and fulfillment, even if it's counterproductive.

The bottom line is that most people are capable, energetic and responsible when given the responsibility. They can plan and schedule. They use their initiative to think of creative solutions. If you don't see it at work but overhear it in the Monday morning conversations, there could be something wrong with the design of the work or the relationship. Harness the talent, or people may find less productive ways to gain some control.

Giving people control over certain aspects of their jobs and permission to make choices about how to proceed has been referred to in popular management literature as empowerment. Since the power must reside somewhere, either with the people or with the bureaucratic rules, organizational policies and orders, empowerment is really a state of mind shared by the employees and their leader. Empowerment is part of an atmosphere stemming from the nature of organizational structure and policy, but also to a large extent from the attitudes and behaviors of the leader. As a leader you may be limited by your organizational policies, but you are not totally powerless in setting the tone.

Empowerment brings results because those results are under the control of the very people who can deliver them. Work to them takes on a deeper meaning. It becomes more than putting in the time and taking home a paycheck. Empowerment leads to ownership and commitment. Mangers don't have to over-manage or micromanage. The employees share a goal, a purpose, which everyone is working toward.

In an empowered organization, leaders consult and make themselves available to help out. You don't find the aloofness and emphasis on levels that are found in many organizations. Everyone is willing to pitch in to get the job done.

This type of environment leads to all kinds of interesting situations:

- Self-managed teams, where daily decisions or necessary coordination is done within a team of 3 to 6 workers. In highly developed cases, these self-managed teams take over most of the work traditionally assigned to a foreman or first-line supervisor.
- Managers assisting on projects, which are led by people who work for them, where they are taking direction from the project leader, a subordinate, who is coordinating all parts of the project. With the popularity of the "do more with less" corporate philosophy, often the manager is the only resource available to do a bit of analysis or other work. The willingness of the boss to participate reinforces the idea that everyone is working together toward the same goal or deadline. This is the essence of Partner Leadership.
- Two-way performance appraisals where managers not only give advice but receive honest feedback from their customers, the employees, about how well they are supporting the common effort.

These kinds of changes do not happen overnight. Experts warn that any culture change is a long-term project and commitment. It can be especially difficult for an individual department within a company with a somewhat different culture. Fortunately it's not an all-or-nothing proposition. Any manager can start small and add responsibility as the trust grows, as the manager gains confidence, and as the people grow into larger personal responsibilities.

What about the risk? There is a risk to trusting people and delegating, but there is a risk to everything in life. You can't stop driving because you might have an accident; you take steps to minimize the risk (defensive driving). Some people will let you down, but my experience and what I overhear on my Monday morning rounds have convinced me that most are capable. They need to be monitored and coached, but not babysat. Tell them what to do and when it's due, but not how to do it (except during training), and usually they will not disappoint. Check often to ensure they are not in over their heads or headed off in a wrong direction. This is when you will be glad you have developed the atmosphere of open communication and good feedback skills. Your people will not be afraid to ask for your help when they need it or are confused or feeling overwhelmed. Then you apply the proper counseling techniques – ask for their help in solving the problem – instead of blaming or dictating your solution.

You can more easily apply this if you have ever been on the other side of such a transaction. Most of us, at one time or another, have worked for someone afraid to take the risk. He will check everything and often redo the work you have done. His subordinates are allowed to make recommendations, but not decisions, about even the most mundane situations. Some call it micromanaging, and we all know it's no fun working in an environment like this. People who act independently in their personal lives resent this loss of autonomy at work. They begin to wonder why the company hired someone with their skill, talent and brains, but fail to take full advantage of them, instead constantly checking and second-guessing. It's frustrating; it decreases trust, respect and motivation. Lack of personal control raises the stress level, just as a feeling of regained control lowers it. In this and many other ways empowerment acts as a motivator.

As seems to be the case in many of these chapters, leaders have a choice. They can exhibit personal confidence and confidence in their people by trusting them with the responsibility, information, tools and leadership to do the job well, or they can make the decisions, give the orders and feel safe. They can face the issues of their own job security and competition, from both peers and subordinates, or they can hoard power and information. Surveys show that the majority of workers don't trust management or even each other, but other studies confirm that leaders who communicate and display strong values will be trusted and will have a loyal following in a crisis. Workers are either controlled by the company/boss or are encouraged to take control of their own job structure and responsibilities. If the bureaucracy, rules, policies and orders control the people, they react with low trust. They are afraid to speak their minds – will even be afraid to tell the truth.

The best leaders take the personal risk in light of the significant payback. They are generous with credit. They seek out highly talented people and welcome them to the team. Then they point people in the right direction and use their leadership skills instead of their power to get the job done. You can't be a great leader, or even a very good manager, if you operate from the standpoint of fear. Fear and perfectionism often go hand in hand driving workers crazy, forcing them to guess what the boss wants instead of what the customer wants.

Ultimately it takes a lot of trust along with self-confidence to put workers in a position to make the right decisions to get the work done. It starts by setting high but realistic expectations and then having the processes in place to monitor progress. It takes clear communication of objectives, deliverables, desired outcomes, but there is a huge payoff for the workers and the managers, and ultimately for the customers and the enterprise as a whole.

By the Numbers

Previous chapters have emphasized the relationship aspects of leadership, but business is primarily about getting results: profits, sales, market share. Since leadership is about getting results through people, it is necessary to shift focus to how these results are measured. It does little good to have good, motivated people when they are not solving the right problems or implementing the right plans. If you don't have measures in place, you don't know where to focus resources and you can't talk about improvement. "Dilbert companies" don't measure enough, don't measure the right things, or don't pay attention to the metrics they have. Their gut informs them about how to make decisions. Before long the employees become frustrated because they are working hard but don't see any progress. Eventually they may lose their jobs due to lack of results, and it's all management's fault.

When it comes to making decisions, many managers like to trust their instincts, and even boast about their preference to do so. It's much easier, and what's the use of having all that experience if you don't use it to solve problems? However, as problems get bigger and more complex, the ability to classify them accurately becomes more difficult. It is a human tendency to categorize new situations and challenges based on previous experiences, but what seems like a comfortable solution that worked in the past may not work in a changing, more interdependent business environment. Worse yet, there is often no concrete, measurable evidence that the old solution or model worked in the first place. It may have merely masked the problem until attention was diverted to the next crisis.

At one time I managed driver training for a large trucking company. One of the terminal training managers called for advice. He was getting pressure from his terminal manger to enhance training with an additional road test after 8 weeks of employment, immediately before drivers were released to begin driving solo. The objective was to reduce accidents in the two months that followed, a critical adjustment period. Since it wasn't part of the curriculum and involved additional resources, I suggested that he run a test by alternating for a few months, road testing every other weekly class of drivers. After four months he sent me his results.

With two groups of drivers and their accident records available on-line, I could do a simple statistical comparison. Two months later when all accident results were available, I had the answer – no difference. Why spend valuable resources – driver time, trainer time, vehicles, fuel, and administrative time – on an activity that yields no results? Measuring and testing this before it was implemented avoided waste. That's the power of data over intuition.

As pointed out in the last chapter, empowerment, the permission to use judgment and skills to get the job done with a minimum of interference or correction from the boss, is a strong motivator. Employees get coaching and objectives and are able to do much of the work on their own; but no matter how good the people are, developing solid objectives is the key to making them (and you) successful. Clear objectives help people decide priorities and plan their time. Objectives define success.

Many sources of management training use SMART as an acronym for the characteristics of good objectives: specific, measurable, action-oriented, realistic, and time-bounded. Tell them what you want, by when, and how it will be measured, knowing that it can be accomplished in that amount of time with the given resources. "I want you to get these results by the end of the month (or the end of the year)." It is crucial that an objective be well defined and measurable, so that at the end of the given period, there is no argument about whether it has been achieved. Don't just talk about improving output, talk about improving from A now to B at some definite time in the future. This also provides the basis for a solid feedback process to discuss rewards or developmental needs based on clear expectations.

Objectives serve a dual function. They set direction and also act as powerful motivators. It's been said that you don't get what you expect; you get what you *inspect*. Measuring something and setting a goal makes it important. It tells people directly what to work on and indirectly what to ignore. Furthermore, if you can't measure it, you can't improve it; and if you don't measure it, you don't know if it has improved. In general, many things can be measured, so the trick is to measure the right things, results and those key performance indicators (KPI) that drive results. Measurements that don't lead to some action or decision are a waste.

Because setting objectives and measuring the important outcomes is crucial, it is important to understand the pitfalls. Since the early use of computers, "garbage in, garbage out" (GIGO) has been the cry of frustrated decision makers. If you don't collect the right data or if information is incomplete or corrupted, no analysis will be worthwhile. Even if information is reasonably complete, the right interpretation is required. If a field is blank, does it mean that it has a zero value or that it should be ignored? What does a negative sale price mean – a return, a cancellation, a rebate, or something else? Often these definitions were created by the people who made the initial entries. Step one is to understand the data.

Managers who don't understand the tools well enough may use the right numbers to come to the wrong conclusions. Following are some examples of how problems arise and how to avoid them in the areas of simple statistical analysis, quality, budgeting, pricing, and experimental design.

With the power of computers, there is never a lack of data. There is usually too much. The best managers figure out how to separate the important from the trivial, but unless you are in a company with elite analytical support, you're on your own. A basic understanding of statistics is important.

Given a data set almost anyone can use a spreadsheet to calculate average and standard deviation. Whenever there is variation, it is useful to know the center of the data and how spread out they are. Of course the average is not always the best measure of location and can be misleading. Median may be more appropriate for a skewed distribution, one that is not evenly balanced. Simply finding the average (or standard deviation) without further consideration can cause erroneous and costly assumptions.

Take for example the earnings of professional athletes. Stars of popular sports make huge sums, in the tens of millions of dollars every year. Others sit on the bench or don't qualify for all the tournaments or play in less lucrative sports. Professional athletes may even include those in the minor leagues or on practice squads. They make thousands of dollars, not millions, and there are many more of them. When trying to judge what the pros earn, a mathematical average, which includes the earning of the stars, can greatly overstate typical earnings. This applies to any other data set that has a few very high or very low elements.

The same spreadsheet applications can also calculate correlation, how two factors vary together. The guiding principle, however, is that correlation does not signify causation. Because two factors vary together does not mean that A causes B. B may cause A, or both may be caused by some other hidden factor. They may be totally unrelated and the appearance of a mathematical relationship may be a random occurrence, a coincidence. If you find a relationship between key measures in your operation that makes sense based on your understanding of the business, this is an important discovery. Validate your assumptions; be sure you can explain the cause and effect relationship between actions and results, i.e., profits, cash flow, or output. This is especially true of non-financial measures as found for example on a balanced scorecard. If you can't show basic causality, you can't identify the important metrics and decide how to allocate resources or set up effective recognition systems.

Deming's and other quality approaches mentioned in Chapter 2 boil down primarily to eliminating waste and maintaining consistency. In business there is always more work to do than there is time to do it. Managers must prioritize by moving what is most important to the top of the list, but first by stopping those activities that don't add value, the waste work. Look for it and eliminate it. Even by eliminating a few needless steps, a whole process can be streamlined and become more efficient.

To further improve a process, it must first be performed consistently. That's what work instructions and control charts are all about. Precision can only be achieved after consistency has been established. The usual analogy is that of shooting bullets at a target. It makes little sense to adjust the sights on a rifle until you are skilled enough to achieve a group of shots close together using the current setting. If all you get is a random spray, sight adjustments guarantee nothing. First get control, a good, steady aim, and then adjust the sights. In the same way consistent results from a machine or any process must precede corrective action.

Novice managers will ask only if a process is in "statistical control." If it is, they seem satisfied – like the work is done. Statistical process control implies only consistent results. It may be consistent, but consistently off target. Because they don't understand the purpose of quality programs fully, they move on to something new, instead of taking that necessary consistency to the next step by trying to move it closer to the bull's eye, the desired performance level.

Budgeting is a traditional practice in the modern business world, with nothing better to replace it; but it has some serious limitations both in design and in application. Current business books and articles stress flexibility and agility, yet budgets in most large companies are fixed, developed in the fall and locked in for the next calendar year. Although it sometimes doesn't make sense, that's the policy and you have to live with it. This initial inflexibility may be amplified by overly strict adherence to the rules causing businesses to miss opportunities.

Ideally, all spending should be thought of as an investment. Money is spent with an expectation of some return. Employees are expected to add more value to the enterprise than their total cost to the employer. Other costs should be held to the same standard. Travel is done to make a sale or enhance customer service for repeat business. Training makes the employees better at their jobs or prepares them for future contributions. If some company were to buy this book, I hope it would be to improve the business by enhancing management skills and not just to spend the training budget. Often, however, this attitude does not carry through. Even top managers will say about a new system or machine or process that it looks good and that they appreciate the savings it will provide, but it has to wait because the purchase price is not in the budget. They forego six months of expected benefits to satisfy a budget requirement. With quick action, agility and flexibility, they could have had the purchase paid off and contributing to the bottom line six months earlier. Instead they wait.

Another example is the holiday party or other company-sponsored celebration. Managers explain that last year was a good year financially, but this year was not, so the party has been cancelled. People are disappointed, but accept the flawed rationale. No company should ever have such a party just as free entertainment. It's an investment in morale or a motivational tool, reward for a job well done. We know from Chapter 6 that people should not be rewarded (or punished) for results they can't influence. So the party should be held because it has an expected payoff. Past financial results have little to do with it unless the company is so small that there is a clear link between individual performance and overall results and the celebration has been set up as a reward. To not reward people because the economy was sour or to reward them only because the economy is good makes no sense from a motivational standpoint. The same reasoning extends to all expenditures. Salespeople may be advised to stay in less fancy hotels when company results are sagging. What comes under scrutiny in bad years should come under the same scrutiny in good years. Investments require a cost/benefit analysis, which is usually independent of past financial performance. If it adds value, do it; otherwise don't. This is not to argue that every minor expense should be justified in the same detail as a capital investment. It is only to point out that too casual treatment leads to decisions driven by budgetary rules or current business climate instead of making good decisions for the future. Likewise, across the board budget cuts are an admission by top management that they don't have a clue about what's happening in their organizations and a slap in the face to every lower level manager who's been acting responsibly. It's the sign of a company with poor measures or lazy management.

Related to budgeting is the idea of cost vs. price. Sometimes the lowest price is not the best deal. Overemphasis on the budget leads managers to make decisions on price instead of cost. When companies identify a cheaper supplier without regard to quality, it costs them more in the long run. These quality-related costs manifest themselves in various ways: more defects, more waste, less reliable deliveries, etc. Short-term decisions based on price often lead to higher overall costs.

Just as understanding statistics and quality is important to good management, so is the understanding of experimental design. Another common practice of less sophisticated companies is to attack a problem by calling a meeting and throwing out ideas. Typical problems are soft sales, an increase in accidents, excessive inventory, employee turnover or a sudden cost increase. After a meeting or brainstorming session, six or seven solutions might be seen as feasible and assigned to individuals or teams for implementation. Everyone optimistically begins planning and making changes. Weeks or months later, if results have improved there is no way to tell which of the ideas worked and which did not. Some may have been more powerful than others, or the counter-productivity of a few may have been masked by the success of the rest. The only way to know for sure is to treat the improvement ideas as experiments. Take one action (treatment) and measure the effects on the problem (the dependent variable), while holding everything else constant as well as possible. Unfortunately this takes patience and focus, which are usually in short supply in a crisis. The television show "Myth Busters" demonstrates this kind of approach very well. It shows how carefully they set up experiments to minimize any external influence, or confounding factor. Then they carefully question the results to make sure they were really testing what they intended to.

Good managers also consider trade-offs. They must answer questions about diminishing returns: is more better; is the payoff worth the added effort and energy? This is nearly impossible without accurate data analysis. One example involves decisions around adding or expanding an Internet sales channel. Customers may shop at the store to get an idea of the look, fit and feel of the product or to ask questions or to make a better comparison with other products. After they have decided, they may finally buy it on-line. Costs that are related to the retail store channel may be associated with the ultimate Internet sale. Conversely, a customer may browse the website before buying at the local store. To measure each channel independently could result in bad decisions. The company would not have taken into account the interplay between these channels. It may be better to only measure the fact that sales have increased after adding the web page and not try to attribute the change to specific activities in any particular sales channel.

Finally, some things are easily measured: profits, output, time delays, and dimensional specifications. Others are more elusive, but it's better to try to measure them than to assume.

Instead of asking how many employees received 40 hours of training, ask what benefits the training yielded. Organizational capabilities, like speed, flexibility, leadership, talent pool, teamwork/collaboration, have been shown to contribute to bottom line results. These are often referred to as intangible assets, but business experts are making efforts to find ways to quantify them. Sometimes this is done through employee surveys, and sometimes through audits conducted by human resource professionals. The object is to link the training effort with some financial or talent improvement.

In an effort to measure things that are difficult to measure directly, companies often rely on surveys as a tool, but surveys can be tricky. How are they administered? Face-to-face interviews are more controlled and can follow up on vague answers, but sacrifice anonymity. It's harder to ensure consistency in wording. Respondents may slant their answers to try to impress the administrators. Even in anonymous surveys or polls people are not totally honest. Sometimes companies send out anonymous surveys to employees hoping for more forthright answers, but they include so many demographic items (department, tenure, sex, etc.) for classification and analysis that employees don't trust the anonymity. Other issues include samples size, rater bias, and inter-rater reliability – does "strongly agree" or "sometimes" mean the same thing to everyone?

Clearly there is a lot to this question of measurement.

A consultant I know received an e-mail from a Six Sigma black belt working for a large US company. Careful analysis of data showed that customers with certain code numbers, those ending in 06, 09, 13, and 15, tended to have more complaints about the quality of service than those with other numbers. The e-mail requested that the party who developed the system for assigning such numbers provide further analysis in order to understand the problem. The customer numbers had been based on geographic location, much like postal codes. Like postal codes no geographic information was contained in the final digits; these were just assigned randomly to distinguish one from another. The Six Sigma analyst understood this and should have known that there was nothing in the system behind assigning the numbers that would explain an increase in complaints; yet, because this was the only correlation he could find, he concluded that the customer numbers must have something to do with the problem. He insisted there must be some hidden information in the data. Six Sigma is a great process with great tools, but it's not about lucky numbers. Sometimes people get so close to the problems and tools used to solve them that they loose the perspective that doing any analysis is really about running the business better.

Measurement is key to running a world-class operation, but it's not measurement for its own sake. Measurement in all these areas counts only if it leads to improved return for the stakeholders of the business: customers, owners and employees. Producing a quality product or service gives customers a better value than they get from the competition and keeps them coming back. Quality practices reduce waste and improve return for the shareholders. Measuring the right things well improves the job satisfaction of the employees and allows managers more time to look at the long-term issues while empowered employees keep the day-to-day business on track. Measurement keeps everyone aligned in the right direction, so they spend their time solving the important problems and anticipating rather than reacting. On the other hand, calculations or predictions based on bad data can lead to confusion, frustration, and wrong decisions. Likewise bad interpretation or conclusions drawn from good data will lead to useless or counterproductive results. More and more in this high-speed global economy, competitors with the most sophisticated analytical tools and talent are the leaders in their respective industries. They don't manage just operations or production by the numbers but also marketing, customer service, logistics, and even some aspects of human resources. Nor all managers have access to sophisticated analytics and expertise to tackle complex problems with optimization, simulation, data mining, or multivariate analysis; but much can be done with spreadsheets, simple modeling, statistical tools, and visualization (graphs, maps and trends).

Much of this chapter relates to the development of incentives as addressed earlier. If you are not measuring the right things in the right way or are making false assumptions, or do not understand the underlying relationships, or are relying on gut feel rather than using data at all, it will lead to poorly designed incentive programs.

In business as in life it's usually impossible to have complete and perfect information. Regardless, decisions must be made. That's where experience comes in. But don't just trust your gut when you have access to better tools, information and analysis.

Putting It All Together

I attended a business conference a few years ago. In the middle of his presentation, a software and project management consultant, after explaining some of the complexities of a particular computer application, stated, "That's why I got out of programming and got into management." Of course it was meant as a joke, but my first thought was that any manager in the room who takes his job seriously ought to be insulted. It was as if programming (or nursing or finance or engineering) is a real skill that requires training and practice, and even special talents, but management is just something you get into when you have either tired of the grind or have reached a level where you can no longer be promoted by staying in the same field. So those trained as programmers are asked to run IT departments, those trained as nurses are put in charge of other healthcare professionals, those with accounting degrees manage finance departments, and a trained engineer may be heading an entire technology company. What do they do when they get there – play it by ear?

In a popular book on interviewing, the author explains the prevalence of bad interviewers in this way: "American business frequently yields to the mistaken belief that any person, on being promoted to the ranks of management, becomes mystically endowed with all necessary management skills."[7] The assumption among many is that it takes no special knowledge or different skill to be a manager. It's just something that you pick up along the way, like parenting skills. Look around for good examples and bad examples and try to model yourself accordingly. Even standard MBA programs spend only a course or two, out of the dozen required, on management or organizational behavior, and these emphasize theory. How

---

7   Martin Yates. Knock 'em Dead 2004. Avon Media, Avon, Massachusetts: 2004. p. 156.

to put that theory into practice in a real, one-on-one situation is apparently left as an exercise to the student.

This is not an assumption shared by just a few. Typical job requirements attest to its widespread nature. A recent job posting on the Internet for a Vice President – Engineering, for example, required an MS in electrical, mechanical or aeronautical engineering. It didn't ask for management skills or education. Either the problems associated with leading and managing people and results are secondary to understanding the technical issues or the former are considered a no-brainer, accessible to anyone with a little bit of experience. (Isn't this a perfect formula for micromanagement?)

Especially in the 1990s during the dot.com boom there were many cases of very good technical people promoted to management based on similar assumptions. Some had the right mix of values and skills and were quite successful. Some were carried along on the wave of technology and the Y2K crisis and were lucky enough to retire before being found out. Others struggled, and the rest were a complete disaster. The ones who suffered the consequences of these bad promotion decisions were the workers most directly, but ultimately the customers and the shareholders.

In the 1960s Laurence Peter developed in a series of books the satirical theory of the Peter Principle. He proposed that the problem with management was that successful people keep getting promoted until reaching a job where they are no longer successful, in over their heads. Then promotion stops. As managers reach their respective "level of incompetence," they stay in that job and continue their mediocre or substandard performance. The people under their control suffer the consequences of the system. Perhaps this is true, or perhaps bad bosses continue to promote those who act and think like them. The overall culture sends the message that those who act this way are the ones who get ahead. The Partner Leadership model is marginalized in favor of tough, results-oriented behavior with a short-term orientation that destroys relationships and sows the seeds of turnover.

Whether the reason for incompetent management is faulty promotion criteria, wrongly oriented job requirements or bad hiring decisions, the problem persists. Pointy-haired bosses beget pointy-haired bosses and the cycle continues.

The solution presented here is built on my 40 years of leadership training and experience in the military and in business, along with all the books, articles, consultants, seminars, advisors and examples – good and bad – that I have been exposed to along the way. My objective has been to consolidate and pass along to new managers, older managers, anyone interested in learning, the core truths behind good leadership, by condensing and sifting through four decades of fads, movements, new initiatives, and management "secrets."

What's left after this distillation is not a long or complex book, but one that forms a comprehensive whole – a way of managing to overcome the (possibly accurate) accusation of running a "Dilbert company" or department. As I warned in the second chapter about some failed attempts to implement other programs, its adoption is not intended to be a cherry-picking exercise. The philosophy and practices are interdependent, building on and relating to each other.

Surveys, media and personal experience indicate rising dissatisfaction among workers in the US. It's a sad situation that affects everyone either as a worker, a customer, or an owner. Cartoons, television shows and movies mocking managerial incompetence remain popular, but in real life poor management is not a laughing matter. Notwithstanding a host of books, articles, seminars and new innovations in business over the past 30 years, the situation seems to have gotten worse. The good news is that the solution is within the control of each manager. In general, direct supervisors have more influence on job satisfaction than any other factor, including pay. But something seems to be lacking.

As is the case in many other fields, the problem is not so much a lack of information. Books, seminars and other guidance abound to the point that competing theories and promises of the easy solution lead to confusion and additional credibility problems for management. Employees and customers seem to understand that there are no magic answers. What's needed is an approach that focuses on and integrates the fundamentals, no-secrets leadership.

Business is about earning a return by serving customers – meeting their needs by delivering something of value at a reasonable price. This is generally done by the workers, not by the managers, whose job it is to facilitate the process. Great leaders truly turn the organization chart upside down. They support their employees treating them like customers whose business needs they must fulfill. This is not meant to imply a buddy-buddy relationship between manager and subordinate. The relationship is one of mutual respect based on honest feedback about business objectives. Both parties understand that high standards and expectations and mutual respect are the norm for working together. This relationship naturally sets the stage for open, honest communications.

Great leaders are skilled communicators and exceptional listeners. A CEO may give great speeches and interviews, but be a terrible communicator with her direct reports. One-on-one communications is the backbone of any relationship both on and off the job. Using good communications, asking for feedback, and really listening leads to the understanding necessary to meet employee needs through goal setting, motivation, performance feedback and change management.

Sincere attempts to inspire or motivate can easily be undermined by poorly designed programs or individual interventions. Rewarding or punishing people for outcomes over which they have no influence will have a negative effect. They become disheartened and disengaged. There must be a clearly understood link between the payoff and some defined, desirable behavior or result.

Good leaders also focus on job-related behavior and results. When things are not going smoothly, they owe it to their employees to give prompt, caring feedback. This consists of a clear description of the problem and its importance, followed by a sincere, mutual attempt to solve it. When things are going smoothly, managers owe it to their employees to reinforce the desired behavior and positive results with a reward, praise, or a simple thank you. Vague references to good work don't count. Any positive feedback must be connected to something the employee can recognize and repeat, or it's wasted. When managers consistently act in this way, employees are never surprised by their year-end reviews. It lowers their stress and makes them more productive.

The same approach can be used for training a new skill as for correcting or continuing current performance. Tell, or preferably show, people what is required. After practice, feedback from the manager or coach will correct, fine tune or reinforce aspects of the training.

Performance feedback is usually not as effective when given to a group. General reminders about what to do or what not to do are wasted on those who don't need them. Commitment is not gained from the offenders. It is better to identify those with a problem and talk directly to them. As I heard one employee say, "I hate to be chewed out in a meeting for something someone else is doing wrong."

Focusing on behavior keeps the conversation away from less concrete topics like attitude. Good managers don't care about or talk about people's attitudes. They focus on whether their behavior meets the short- and long- term needs of the customers and the organization. If employees find certain customers irritating or difficult, it doesn't matter as long as they consistently treat them respectfully.

The same behavioral approach extends to change management. Discuss the problem, the need for change in an honest and constructive way. There is no need for threats; the threats are built into the business environment. Describe the desired state as contrasted with the present state along with the path to get there. Accept help when it is offered. Even a bad idea is an opportunity to re-explain and reinforce the situation.

All of the previous practices will begin to establish an atmosphere of trust and mutual respect between the workers and their leader. There is a business to run, projects to complete, deadlines to meet, and everyone is in it together in partnership. People must be working on the right things and know what success looks like. Measurable goals and objects are set, but the analysis and experiments are only tools. They lead to decisions and action. Anyone can buy or lease the same factories, warehouses, or computer software. Those alone will not deliver sustainable competitive advantage. The real strength of the organization, its competitive advantage, comes from its people and from the leaders' abilities to get everyone aligned to deliver those results to the best of their abilities. There is ample evidence that this type of culture and behavior leads to superior performance.

Companies that value the three key groups: shareholders, customers and employees, will be successful in the long term. The shareholders are satisfied by growth and profitability. This depends on having happy customers, repeat customers, customers who tell their colleagues, relatives and friends what a great value they get from doing business with your company. This in turn depends on having well-trained and motivated employees – employees who understand and are constantly working toward satisfying customers. It requires leaders to reflect these values, managers who marry the idea of leadership and management with the idea of stewardship and partnership toward a common goal. Those who see themselves as stewards, instead of bosses, will choose responsibility over entitlement and accountability over power. They will choose service over self-interest. They will remember W. Edward Deming's point 7: The aim of supervision should be to help people and machines and gadgets to do a better job.

For most, this is truly a culture change. It has a different look and feel, different cultural artifacts. As an example, the traditional manager sets himself up as a customer, as the one to be pleased. Instead of using increased computer capability to increase the stakeholder benefits, valuable time is invested in managers giving fancy presentations to each other and to their bosses. The customer-manager feels good about professional-looking color slides and that everyone went to so much trouble to prepare a good presentation for him. A really effective leader would ask why so much time and resources were spent on an internal presentation. In too many cases, the dog-and-pony shows trump true results; it's the victory of presentation over substance. Those who choose traditional management care more about themselves than about any of the three groups above. Their focus is apparent to the whole organization and negatively influences the choices others make when doing their jobs. In a well-run company there is a certain consistency that makes everyone more effective and less stressed. You never hear people asking what kind of mood the boss is in. It's not about the boss, it's about the customers, and that message is lived out everyday by everyone – especially the boss.

Good leaders select for talent, set clear goals and measureable objectives, reward meeting those objectives, give their people the support they need to be successful and then let them do their jobs. Be aware there is personal risk involved. This is not necessarily the kind of behavior that gets people promoted today. I have seen some leaders who would be the model for the villain of a story composed by their employees or even their customers. They go about their day-to-day business oblivious to the fact that they are barriers to progress and in some cases even detrimental. They are like the people who drive below the speed limit in the left lane of the interstate apparently not noticing or caring that everyone is forced to pull around them. They are fat and happy and not likely to change because their superiors do not confront their negative effects on the business. They keep trying the "solutions" discussed in Chapter 2 and wonder why they don't work. But they won't be around forever.

As a leader you are in a position to make jobs either truly interesting or boring and unrewarding. At first this may seem hard to believe, but I think of all of the people who are drawn to the theaters to see a good action or adventure movie. A job may not be as exciting and romantic as one of those movies, but it can certainly share some of the key characteristics. Take James Bond as an example. He is given a clear assignment, "this is the bad guy; figure out what he is up to and stop him." He is given the tools to do it with, a special watch or a car with missiles and a smoke screen. When he meets up with a situation that he is not equipped to handle, he is expected to use his ingenuity to arrive at a solution that brings him closer to his objective. Then his bosses, for the most part, get out of his way and let him do his job, supporting him when necessary with reinforcements or the latest information. They also complement him on a job well done and critique his failure to follow approved procedures or to care for his tools, especially the car that often ends up being destroyed. Now I don't expect that business leaders would be able to tell their workers, "Here's your assignment and you leave on the next flight to Zurich." But I know that someone who is given a clear objective, the tools to accomplish it, the support when needed, and timely feedback will feel a lot more like James Bond than the same worker who does not understand what is expected, does not get the support, and has the supervisor telling him what to do or not do at every turn.

Let's build a business climate where the workers of tomorrow are treated better than the workers of today, a business climate that makes people consider those cartoons like Dilbert or television and movies with the theme of a poorly managed office archaic, unrealistic and out of touch. After all, many of us will remain the employees of the future in one way or another. Certainly we will be the customers of the future. With so many people depending on 401(k)s, union pension plans and personal investments for retirement, we are also the shareholders of the future. It is in everyone's best interest that small businesses, non-profits and corporations of the future, and even every department within those corporations, be run by the best managers and leaders, guiding satisfied workers who will deliver more value to those customers and those shareholders. These companies will be much stronger as measured by employee loyalty, increased productivity, high quality, customer satisfaction, and overall value created by really well run organizations.

Why is there Dilbert? It is time that every leader, executive, manager, supervisor looked in the mirror to answer that question.

About The Author

James Jeray is a graduate of the US Military Academy at West Point and holds master's degrees in business from the University of Wisconsin – Oshkosh and in administrative science from the University of Wisconsin – Green Bay. After completing active duty service he spent the next 35 years as a manager and director in the logistic industry with assignments in human resources, training, operations, procurement, engineering and consulting.

Over the course of his career he has encountered many examples of both good and bad leadership. He feels passionately that the so-called secrets promoted in books and seminars have given business leaders false hope and the misconception that some magic bullet can replace the fundamentals. The result has been an erosion of employee satisfaction, mediocre customer service and sub-standard organizational performance.

Mr. Jeray is currently retired, living in Lafayette, IN with his wife, Marilyn.

References

Below are a few of the articles and books that influenced the writing of this book, beyond those that appear in chapter footnotes.

Abrahamson, Eric. "Change without Pain." Harvard Business Review July-August 2000.
Amabile, Teresa M. and Kramer Steven J. "Inner Work Life: Understanding the Subtext of Business Performance." Harvard Business Review May 2007.
Blake, R. & Mouton, J. The Managerial Grid: The Key to Leadership Excellence. 1964.
Block, Peter. "Empowering Employees." Training and Development Journal April 1987.
Bodek, Norman. "The Gemba Walk." Quality Digest February 2004.
Charam, Ram. "Lead by Putting Purpose Before Self." www.finance.yahoo.com December 7, 2006.
Coombes, Andrea. "Show me you care." www.marketwatch.com October 21, 2007.
Demings, W. Edwards. Out of the Crisis. 1986.
Drucker, P. "How to Make People Decisions." Harvard Business Review July-August 1985.
Filipczak, Bob. "Obfuscation Resounding: Corporate Communication in America." Training July 1995.
Goffee, Robert and Jones, Gareth. "Why Should Anyone Be Led by You?" Harvard Business Review September-October 2000.
Heifetz, Ronald A. and Laurie, Donald. "The Work of Leadership." Harvard Business Review December 2001.
Hertzberg, Frederick. "One More Time: How do you Motivate Employees?" Harvard Business Review January-February 1968.
Jeray, James. "Monday Morning Quarterback." The Performance Advantage December 2000.
Jeray, James. Statistics: Short and Simple. 2003.
Johnson, Cynthia Reedy. "An outline for Teambuilding." Training January 1986.
Livingston, J. Sterling. "Pygmalion in Management." Harvard Business Review July-August 1969.

McGregor, D. "An Uneasy Look at Performance Appraisals." Training and Development Journal June 1987.
Offerman, Lynn R. "When followers Become Toxic." Harvard Business Review January 2004.
Paton, Scott M. "The Next Big Thing." Quality Digest April 2004.
Reynolds, Peter C. "Imposing a Corporate Culture." Psychology Today March 1997.
Rosenbluth, Hal and Peters, Diane Mcferrin. The Customer Comes Second. 1992.
Sashkin, Marshall. Managing Conflict Constructively. 1989.
Schein, Edgar. Organizational Culture and Leadership. 1992.
Wetlaufer, Suzy. "Who Wants to Manage a Millionaire?" Harvard Business Review July-August 2000.

www.ingramcontent.com/pod-product-compliance
Lightning Source LLC
Chambersburg PA
CBHW030904180526
45163CB00004B/1694